Aruban Escape

A Samantha Rose Novel

The adventures of 2 young women while on vacation in Aruba.

A novel by Emmanuelle St. Jacques

All rights reserved. Under the U.S. Copyright Act of 1976, the scanning, uploading, and electronic sharing of any part of this book without permission of the publisher is unlawful piracy and theft of the

Thank you for your support of the author's rights

Other than those acknowledged in the foreword, all characters and events in this book are fictitious and from the imagination of the author. Any similarity to real persons, living or dead, is coincidental and not intended by the author.

.

Website: grayauthor.com

© **Copyright registered (2025) John H Gray**

ISBN Number: ISBN 978-1-0692564-0-9

Foreword

One of the difficulties in writing this book and setting it in the small Island of Aruba was to respect the Island, while incorporating fictional drama, romance, and events, along with integrating some real-life people and situations. Another consideration was that of writing a novel with a plot, and not having it become a travelogue.

There are several individuals I would like to thank. Ewald Biemans, Bucuti and Tara Resort, Alexander Goeting, Dushi Tera Experience, Carla Cavallaro Jolly Pirates, Wilmer Quero Costa Linda. Also, Lissa Gray for her eagle-eyed proofing, and Val Berg for comments and suggestions. There are probably others whom, if I omitted them, I apologize.

The Island of Aruba is a special place with an interesting population comprised of many different nationalities that add to its charm and character. Those differences are evident in the foods, music, and culture.

For a small island in the Caribbean that is reliant on tourism, Aruba has many achievements. The education and drive that is shown in life, where people speak multiple languages...Dutch, Papiamento, Spanish, and English. Arubans demonstrate a natural curiosity and interest in others.

A special place for many.

Part 1

A not-so-ordinary day for Samantha

Chapter 1

Challenges

At 36 years of age, Samantha Rose had garnered an excellent reputation for the meticulous legal victories she had achieved at the elite Chicago-based cut-throat law firm of Gouge, Driller, and Hammer. While predominantly a male-dominated preserve where the male partners exercised a combination of power, influence, and participation over the business, this was often at the exclusion of the women partners and juniors. Samantha had thrived. Her tenacity and professional attitude made her unassailable.

Tall and slender with her long, dark hair tightly pulled back, Samantha's striking features and posture exuded a natural yet professional image. Despite this image, her occasional insecurity showed in the form of chewed nails or flicking of her lip.

The daughter of a decorated Naval officer who died mysteriously, Samantha had channelled her grief into academic excellence and graduated top of her class at the prestigious University of Chicago Law School. The immense inheritance he left her did not diminish the grief she felt.

Financially independent, Samantha was fiercely loyal to her small group of friends, though at times she felt guilty about her advantage.

She snapped out of daydreaming when the office administrator dropped a large manila envelope on her desk.

Samantha froze, looking at the mysterious envelope on her desk. She questioned whether to open it or just continue ignoring it. Curiosity won out, and she snatched up the envelope. Fearing the worst, and wondering what new legal assault her ex, Terry Steele, and his repugnant lawyer had contrived. She tore it open. Instead, it was a letter from a disgruntled client filled with profanities and obscene suggestions. She crunched up the letter and threw it in the wastebasket.

The day had been filled with challenges and nastiness. Emotionally, she was unable to withstand any further confrontations. Not wanting to create a scene with anyone, she grabbed her coat and decided to leave the office early. She wanted to be home in the warmth and security of her own space. Her mind filled with the memory of the trip she had taken with Terry Steele to Hawaii. She had loved the beauty of the island and wished there was another trip planned to take her away from all the pressures of work.

Dark grey clouds filled the sky. Bitterly cold north winds blew off Lake Michigan and howled through the tall canyons of Chicago's downtown buildings. The streets were busy. Christmas shoppers braved the elements in a last-minute frenzy to find that special gift.

Samantha exited the high-rise that housed the law firm of Gouge, Driller, and Hammer. The firm, founded in 1978 by Richard Gouge, James Driller, and William Hammer, quickly established national recognition and became a formidable presence in Chicago.

Specializing in business litigation, trust management, and corporate acquisitions, Samantha enjoyed the constant challenges the firm offered.

Occupying the top 5 floors of the prestigious King's House office building, the senior partners' offices offered magnificent views of Lake Michigan and Chicago's skyline. Samantha's successes warranted an office of equal elegance. This infuriated Terry Steele, and he was determined to change that.

Her day at work had been anything but festive or enjoyable. As a junior lawyer, she was normally assigned monotonous and boring cases. Except for the current case. A difficult one. The day had been spent researching statutes involving legal standings between the State and Municipal governments.

Out on the street, Samantha pulled up the high collar of her heavy, deep blue woolen coat and shielded her face and ears from the cold, wet, blowing snowflakes. While she enjoyed the Christmas and New Year period, she hated the accompanying weather that occurred at that time of year.

She clasped her tan leather attaché case tight to her chest, while her other hand protected her purse. She gingerly navigated the slippery snow-covered pavement, her mid-calf insulated boots sliding on icy patches.

Other pedestrians occasionally bumped into her shoulder as they attempted to hurry past her on the narrow sidewalk. This increased her frustration and added to her gloomy mood, caused by the day's incidents and him, Terry Steele. She silently cursed her stupidity for having allowed the brief romance with Terry Steele, the wonder boy of the firm.

Terry Steele. A complex mix of charm and manipulation, Terry Steele projected both confidence and authority, yet carefully hid his deep character flaws. At 41 years of age, Terry Steele had risen through Chicago's legal elite. He was an athletic, good-looking lawyer who had made a full partnership at an early age. He was as brilliant as he was charming. At 6 feet tall, with permanently tanned features, dressed in expensive, tailored suits, a dazzling smile, and a magnetic personality that oozed charm, both men and women were captured and intrigued by him.

Terry Steele spoke with practiced precision and switched between charming persuasion and legal expertise to psychologically manipulate both clients and his partners.

He was a natural leader, and it showed.

Samantha had been enraptured by him when she was a young articling lawyer at the firm. He had focused his attention on her, and she had melted. An intense affair had developed, and Samantha believed she had found her life partner.

Working at the firm, with him present every day, had been heaven until their romance crashed in a spectacular fashion. For the months after, Samantha suffered and even sought psychological assistance to deal with the rejection and loss of confidence. Throughout their relationship, Samantha had watched as his attention moved to other aspects of life, often at her expense. The final and deciding factor had been an argument. Samantha had planned a special romantic evening to celebrate their first anniversary that weekend. Terry Steele dismissed it as a self-serving event for her satisfaction and was keeping his plans for a 3-day golf holiday in the Bahamas with friends. She had pleaded with him to reschedule his trip, but his response was a final refusal in which he insulted and belittled her.

Eventually, Samantha was able to dismiss the feelings of the past and focus on her legal career. Terry Steele decided to manipulate situations in the firm to force her resignation or firing. She realized his behavior and resisted it, even if it meant putting in extra effort on the cases she handled. This, to her satisfaction, infuriated him.

With her mind recalling the affair, Samantha passed by the decorative shop windows, unaware of their brightly lit Christmas displays or hearing the festive sounds of the piped-out Carols playing on speakers at the store entrances.

She continued her walk to the Chicago Transit Authority bus stop, where she found over a hundred other commuters huddled against the cold, waiting for one of the continually late and overcrowded buses.

The piercing winds penetrated her thick coat and chilled her chest. Samantha surveyed the waiting crowd and decided to forgo the bus and treat herself to a cab. She walked away from the bus stop and attempted to wave down a yellow taxi that was stopped at the traffic lights. The lights changed, and the taxi sped towards her. Instead of stopping, it passed her while spraying slushy snow and water over the front of her, soaking her already wet coat. She braved the situation and attempted to flag down another taxi, but to no avail. All the taxis sped by. Despondent, she returned to the bus stop and waited.

Thirty minutes passed before a crowded bus arrived. She pushed herself forward amongst a throng of others boarding the bus. There were no seats, and she stood and was jostled along with other wet passengers. The smell of body odor, wet clothing, and fast food permeated the air. Samantha could not wait until the forty-minute ride was over and she could exit the commuter hell.

The bus ground to a halt near her Oak Grove apartment. Samantha breathed a sigh of relief and elbowed her way off the bus. Within minutes, she arrived at her condo, The Walden Tower.

The Walden Tower was a recently constructed building containing luxurious units. Marketing of the residences was targeted at young professionals who could afford the price of luxury.

Jefferson, the doorman, quickly threw open the large glass entrance door for her as she approached. The wind howled through the door's opening gap, and some dead leaves that had fallen during autumn spun in an eddy and blew into the building.

"Good evening, Miss Rose. Horrible weather this evening. A good night to enjoy being home in the warmth."

Samantha acknowledged him and proceeded across the expensive beige marble-floored foyer to the elevators. A large, beautiful Christmas tree adorned the entrance and greeted the residents and visitors with its twinkling, soft lights and decorations. As she passed the concierge desk, Lionel, the concierge, called out to her.

"Evening, Miss Rose. There is a courier envelope for you. It was delivered late this afternoon."

Samantha held a special place in her heart for Lionel. Even though he was a man with limited academic education, Lionel was always meticulous and professionally courteous. He addressed Samantha with utmost respect and seemed to anticipate her needs.

She looked at him closely. He was in his mid-fifties with salt and pepper hair, dressed in his impeccably pressed charcoal uniform with his reading glasses hanging from a cord around his neck.

At the desk, she signed for the envelope and examined it, wondering who had sent it to her home address. The large manila envelope had no markings or identification. Her name and address were printed on an expensive label. She assumed it was probably another demand from Terry Steele's attorney for the property he claimed that he had left at her condo, even though there was none. She stuffed the envelope under her arm and walked to the elevator, muttering profanities under her breath.

Samantha rode the elevator up to her 10th-floor $2.4 million penthouse condo. She had treated herself to the luxury of the condo upon achieving full partnership and with the inheritance she had received after the death of her father. Captain Owen Rose.

US Navy Captain Rose, a decorated officer, had been a man of both complex discipline and human warmth. His integrity and professionalism resulted in the Navy assigning him to multiple classified operations.

Captain Owen Rose had been killed on his final mission in 2015. The mission, a mysterious assignment, was secret and heavily classified. Only fragments of information leaked from the heavily redacted documents.

Eager to keep the sophisticated mission secret, the US Navy had been overly generous in settling with the family, who in turn agreed to conditions of secrecy and silence. The Navy did not want any publicity regarding the mission Captain Rose was commanding. It pained Samantha that her decorated father's outstanding career was to be buried in this manner. For all purposes, the Navy deemed he never existed.

Not to be deterred by the US Navy's attitude, Samantha and her mother decided to respect his heritage and honor his wishes. Captain Rose had been born and raised in St Andrews, Scotland. They arranged a traditional Scottish funeral in his hometown of St Andrews, historically known for its golf courses and seaside charm.

The funeral was attended by a larger number of his relatives and included a procession, with a bagpiper; a service with hymns, readings, and eulogies. There was a wake after the service. Respecting his lifelong love of the sea, a seaside ceremony was later held after his cremation to scatter his ashes.

Upon reaching her condo, Samantha removed the integrated electronic control from her purse. The building owners had spared no expense in installing top-of-the-line residential security systems in each suite. Samantha heard the click of the door unlocking and the soft chirp as the security system disarmed.

Floor-to-ceiling windows framed spectacular views of Chicago. The 3200 square foot space was normally flooded with natural light; however, today's weather conditions had dimmed the interior but made the view from the windows more pronounced. The floors were Italian marble, and her chef's kitchen was equipped with modern custom cabinetry.

She was barely in the door when Horace, her feisty Siamese cat, ran to greet her. The troubles of the day started to melt away as she soaked in the ambiance of her prized home. The cat's purring and rubbing against her raised her spirits.

Horace was a striking seal point Siamese with deep blue eyes. He possessed a classic Siamese personality, which was demanding, vocal, and imperious. He was 7 years old and had been adopted from a shelter 3 years earlier by Samantha. Initially, he had rebelled, but finally adapted and claimed the whole condo as his domain. He was skeptical of visitors and examined them from his favorite perch in front of the gas fireplace.

As she entered, she observed her reflection in the antique gold-framed full-length mirror. She was horrified at the condition of her coat. It was soaked, and the spray from the taxi had contained mud and dirt, which had stained her front. Samantha frowned at the brownish matter on the arm. She assumed it was ketchup or some other indescribable spill from the fast food that some of the other passengers on the bus were eating. She took off the coat and threw it into her bathroom, where she could safely fold it to take to the dry cleaners. She did not want to drip water from the coat through her condo.

Horace was demanding food and followed her to the kitchen while meowing loudly. She filled his silver bowl with Blue Ribbon Premium Holistic Niblets.

With Horace fed and a quiet evening ahead, Samantha decided to take a shower in her rainforest-themed shower. For twenty minutes, she stood under the soft, warm shower and enjoyed the experience of the pulsating side jets as they massaged her sides and back.

After her shower, she dressed in her thick terry robe and returned to the living room. She flicked on her rustic gas fireplace and went to the kitchen to pour a long glass of Chablis.

The living area warmed quickly from the gas fire. Samantha dropped back onto the thick white leather couch and sank into the large cushions. She closed her eyes and thought of the day, and in particular, the case she had been assigned to by the firm's partners. She knew it would be an unwinnable case as the State government and Municipal government had conflicting policies, and the client would never win. She realized this was another ploy from Terry Steele to belittle her in front of the other partners. She intended to meet the client the next afternoon and suggest an alternative building application that would, in all probability, be approved. It was a small change and one that had been overlooked by Terry Steele and the others. She intended to win.

Horace jumped up onto the couch and attempted to head-butt her. Samantha recoiled. The strong tunalike smell on his breath from the cat food was nauseating and not something that went with her wine. She gently pushed him away.

Finally, a feeling of serenity settled within her. The room was warm. A soft yellow flame flickered from the fire. A soft, low jazz played.

Feeling melancholy, Samantha looked at the mysterious envelope and questioned whether to open it or just continue to enjoy the mood. Curiosity won out, and she snatched up the envelope.

Fearing the worst and wondering what new legal assault Terry Steele and his deranged lawyer had contrived, she ripped it open.

Inside was another envelope bearing the logo for her bank. Her name was written by hand on the face of the envelope. It was written in the finest calligraphy. Samantha's curiosity piqued. She gently opened it and removed the single folded sheet of paper. It was the personalized stationery of the Vice President of Customer Relations at the Head Office of her bank, The Communal National Bank. It was a simple greeting and a request to call Mr. Clive Jonas at his direct number to arrange an important meeting.

Samantha frowned and placed the envelope and letter back on the coffee table. She wondered if it was something to be worried about. She cast her mind back to recent interactions with the bank. There were no issues she could recall. She picked up the letter and reread it. She glanced over at her kitchen clock. The evening was still early, and she wondered if Mr. Clive Jonas was still at his office. She decided to take a risk and call the number. The phone was answered on the third ring.

"Clive Jonas. How may I assist?"

"Good evening. This is Samantha Rose. I received a letter from you requesting that I call you."

"Yes, indeed. Thank you for your fast response. Now, without causing you concern or creating a mystery, I am inviting you to come to the bank and meet with me. It will all be clear then. Can we meet soon?"

"I have appointments tomorrow afternoon with a special client, and then I am off out of the city to visit my mother for the Christmas break. I plan on spending a few weeks with her after the loss of her husband. This is a difficult time."

"Are you available tomorrow morning? I will send a bank driver to pick you up and take you back after we meet."

Intrigued by the situation, Samantha agreed, and they arranged an early meeting.

After the call, Samantha reflected on her knowledge of the bank. The Communal National Bank was one of Chicago's premier financial institutions and was headquartered in an impressive heritage building in downtown Chicago.

Samanatha's relationship with the bank spanned many years. In her student days, she had banked there and, after her father's death, had worked with them in setting up the trust accounts for the family.

After the call, she refreshed her wine and returned to the couch and sat, wondering what was ahead. Within a few minutes, and from the effect of the wine, she started to tire. Samantha stood and went to her beautifully appointed bedroom. Sleep came quickly.

Chapter 2

A different day

Samantha awoke from her deep sleep feeling refreshed. Horace leaped up onto her bed to ensure he was not forgotten and would be fed before she made coffee or performed any other task.

With a coffee in hand, Samantha crossed the living area, looked outside, and saw the heavy snowfall of giant wet snowflakes. She flipped on the TV news. Good Morning America hosts droned on about recent political events in Washington, which she found boring. As she was preparing her breakfast, GMA paused, and the local TV station cut in. The female host made an exaggerated effort to announce the local weather conditions and their impact. Her cohost shook his head as she rhymed off the cancellations of trains, the closure of schools, and the suspension of sports events and other functions. Samantha was concerned. She needed to get to her meeting with Mr. Clive Jonas at the bank. Concerned, she decided to call him.

"Mr. Jonas, this is Samantha Rose. I am wondering if we should reschedule our meeting given the weather situation."

"No, not at all. Our driver is already on the way to pick you up. I understand you may get a little delayed due to the weather and traffic conditions, but that is fine. I look forward to our meeting. We will be waiting."

Samantha disconnected and frowned. He has said WE. She had expected just Clive Jonas at the meeting. She hurriedly went to the bathroom and checked her appearance and makeup. Some premonition caused her to believe that the meeting was for something special. Maybe the bank wanted to offer her a position. She dismissed that thought. Why would a VP of Customer Relations be involved in that?

The security system intercom beeped, and Lionel, the concierge, announced that a driver was waiting for her. Samantha wrapped her faux fur-lined leather coat around her, gathered her purse and attaché case, and left for her appointment.

In the lobby, maintenance staff were busy drying the wet, melted snow from the marble floor. Samantha carefully maneuvered her way toward the door. Lionel left his desk and came to her assistance, helping her retain her balance and not slip. The driver stood holding a large, folded umbrella. He was an immense man who stood over 6 feet tall. He flashed a smile at Samantha and reached to escort her to the car while spinning the umbrella in his other hand, causing it to open.

He sheltered Samantha from the heavily falling wet snow.

"Good morning, Miss Rose. I am Henry and will be your driver for the day. Mr. Jonas has asked me to drive you wherever you need to go after your meeting. It will be my pleasure. With this terrible weather, it is best that you don't take the transit buses or train."

"That is very kind. I will go to my office after the meeting. It's not far, so I don't think I will need your service. Thank you, though."

"Haha. If I don't look after you as told, I will be in serious trouble. Consider this. I am your chauffeur for the day."

"But, I don't plan on traveling very far today. Just to my office and then back to my home."

"Miss, why don't you wait until after you meet with Mr Jonas to decide that?"

"Henry, do you know something about the reason for the meeting? What is going on? What is it about?"

"Miss Rose, you must wait. Don't be impatient. Mr. Jonas is a nice gentleman. You have nothing to worry about."

She found Henry to be warm and attentive. His demeanor had been shaped by years of service as a military police officer. At 6'2" and with a solid build, it was obvious to Samantha that his role was more than just a driver. The bank had hired him because of his stature as a skilled and effective security officer.

Samantha settled comfortably in the rear seat of the limousine. She watched as Henry masterfully worked his way through the congested snowy roads and onto the freeway. The traffic crawled at a slow pace behind a group of snowplows operating beside each other and preventing anyone from passing.

Her curiosity piqued. She had tried to find any possible reason why an officer of her bank would request such a strange meeting. Unable to identify any cause, she gave up.

Henry slightly increased the warmth in the limousine and played some soft and smooth jazz. It helped calm Samantha as she had felt a mild anxiety increasing. She hoped there was nothing serious that required the meeting.

Horns blared as they approached the exit ramp down into the area where the bank's head office was located. Drivers jockeyed for space to exit, and through the car windows, and from the facial expressions and hand gestures, Samantha could make out the frustration and swearing. There was nothing like a good Chicago snowfall at peak traffic hours to bring out the best in people, she thought.

Henry smoothly navigated across several lanes and down the exit ramp. Upon reaching the main street, he turned into a hidden entrance and activated the garage door with his remote control. Within seconds, they were in the depths of the bank's multi-storey building. He pulled over to an area reserved for executives. A door hid the private elevator to the executive offices.

Henry exited the driver's seat, opened the door, and escorted Samantha to the elevator. The ride was short. The elevator stopped at the ground floor of the building, and a security officer checked her ID and bags before releasing the elevator to continue its ascent to the corporate suites.

The ride was smooth and silent. They stopped on the 12th floor. Henry stood back as Samantha exited. A jovial middle-aged woman greeted them.

"Miss Rose. Welcome. Let me show you to Clive's office. He is eager to meet you."

Samantha was further confused. She had never met him, nor could she recall any interaction with him.

"I am confused. What is happening? My only business with the bank is my investment and savings account. Is there some problem?"

"No, my dear, have some patience. It will be explained soon."

The woman stopped and gently knocked on a large mahogany door. It was opened by a silver-haired man who seemed to have a permanent smile etched on his face. He thrust his hand forward.

"Miss Rose. I am Clive Jonas. I am pleased to meet you. Come and sit. I trust Henry drove you safely. Would you care for a cappuccino? I love them in the morning."

Clive Jonas was in his mid-fifties. His face expressed a warmth, and crinkled smile lines accentuated his piercing steel blue eyes.

Samantha sat on a long couch. His desk faced Lake Michigan.

"Mr. Jonas, I am nervous and do not understand what this is all about."

In a confident and reassuring tone, Clive Jonas attempted to gain her confidence.

"Please be calm. Enjoy your coffee while I learn a little about you."

Confused and cautious, Samantha described a little about herself and her career.

The cappuccino coffees arrived accompanied by a plate of Biscotti.

Clive served a coffee to her and offered the cookies. Samantha started to relax. She noticed Clive Jonas looking at his watch every few minutes. It seemed as if he was expecting something to happen.

For what seemed like hours, Samantha and Clive Jonas sat making small talk until there was another knock at the door. Clive opened it, and a small, young woman entered.

"Miss Rose, I would like to introduce you to Tracy Brown. Tracy is the Director of the firm who handles all of the bank's public relations."

"Please don't call me Miss Rose. I prefer Samantha."

"Well, OK. Let us get on with it, shall we? First, let me get Tracy a coffee as well."

Clive motioned for them all to take seats on the couch and the accompanying club chairs.

"I am going to let Tracy explain why we called you here for this meeting."

"Samantha, our firm always searches for ideal promotions for The Communal National Bank. It is in the bank's code of ethics to promote and participate with citizens of Chicago who are also customers of the bank. Recently, we ran a promotion for the bank. You might be aware of the promotion. It has been running for months. We started it in the fall when the weather was changing, and offered a prize of a warm Caribbean trip that would appeal to the bank's customers.

The promotion randomly selected certain customers who had various financial products at the bank. You were selected as the winner of the main prize. Congratulations. Now it is with pleasure that Clive will describe the prize."

Samantha sat speechless and in shock. She recalled filling in some entry form, but had dismissed it from her mind. She never won prizes in lotteries or otherwise.

After the gloom of yesterday, she was not expecting better things to happen today.

Clive returned to his desk. He removed a leather folder monogrammed with the bank's logo from a credenza behind his desk. He picked up his desk phone and punched in several numbers.

"Yes, Mr. Hutton, she is here. If you could join us, please."

"Samantha, Mr. Hutton is the President of the bank. He will join us to present the prize. We also request your permission and agreement to allow Tracy to have her photographer record this. We will use the picture for publicity to demonstrate our commitment to the community."

"Yes, of course. I am so curious to know what the prize is, though."

The office door opened, and a young man entered. He was introduced by Clive as Mr. Hutton. Samantha was shocked. She had expected a much older person, but instead, a polished young athletic man in his thirties joined them. Samantha felt a flutter. He was both handsome and courteous. He walked over to Samantha and took her hand, and raised it to his lips to kiss it.

"Please don't think I am too forward, but it truly is a pleasure to meet you. My name is Hutton, but please call me Peter."

Samantha blushed and dropped her head slightly.

Clive crossed the room from his desk and handed the folder to Tracy, and as he did so, he spoke directly to her.

"Samantha, you seem surprised. Mr. Hutton is a unique member of the normally staid community of bank presidents. Mr Hutton introduced a series of innovative new approaches to banking and has earned an enviable reputation in the banking community.

Now, Tracy, stand with Mr. Hutton to Samantha's side, and I will stand on the other side for your photographer to capture Mr. Hutton handing the folder with the prize to her."

As the photographer snapped pictures, Mr. Hutton handed the maroon-colored folder to Samantha and spoke.

"Samantha, on behalf of The Communal National Bank, we are pleased to hand you this prize. You and a companion have won a 10-day First Class all-expense paid trip to the magical Caribbean Island of Aruba.

First, Samantha was shocked, and then tears welled in her eyes. After all of her recent troubles, she was in disbelief.

Chapter 3

Decisions

After a brief congratulatory session in Mr. Clive Jonas' office, Samantha, still in shock, made some decisions. Before leaving his office and the bank, she asked to use a phone. She was shown into a small private office.

Before she could make her calls, Tracy Brown asked to join her. Tracy explained that Samantha would need to arrange a meeting with her and the company in charge of organizing the trip. Tracy advised her that she would need to obtain copies of her passport and other documents. She advised Samantha that she would send a list of the required documents, along with details of the events in Aruba that were included with the prize.

Tracy left, and Samantha sat in silence, thinking of the sudden change to her plans. She hated the cold winter of Chicago, and the idea of a Caribbean break appealed to her immensely. Samantha knew very little about Aruba, other than it was part of the Dutch Kingdom and located near Venezuela in the Caribbean. She intended to research the island upon returning to her condo.

The combination of excitement and shock distorted Samantha's otherwise sharp mind. She decided and phoned her Executive assistant at the law firm to cancel all her appointments for the day, including with the client for whom she had been preparing the submission to the court over the conflicting government statutes.

She asked her Executive assistant to reschedule him for the next day.

Still excited, she tried to call her best friend, Sophia Wright.

Her Moroccan friend, Sophia, an effervescent extrovert with a natural optimism. Her recent divorce had left her with emotional scars, but also a renewed appreciation of the loyalty of her true friends.

At 34, Sophia radiated a vitality with her frequent laugh and gentle teasing. Coupled with her curly auburn hair, hazel eyes, and friendly demeanor, she easily befriended others.

To match her personality, Sophia's wardrobe consisted of brightly colored pieces, both modern and vintage.

Samantha loved Sophia and valued the friendship.

The phone continued to ring unanswered.

Samantha found that confusing, as Sophia operated a home office and had frequent contact with her customers. After a while, she called again. This time, the phone was answered.

"Sophia, how are you? I tried calling, but the phone wasn't answered. Are you OK?"

"Oh yes. I needed to take a long pee, girl. You know how it is after too much morning coffee."

Samantha smiled. She liked that Sophia was so honest and straightforward.

"Sophia, something has happened to me. I need to see you."

"What? Are you pregnant? Is that slimeball Terry Steele creating more problems? I'd love to cut his balls off. What is it? Are you OK? Should I come over?"

"No, and no to all of that. Yes, I want to see you. How about an early lunch? I will come by in my limo and pick you up. Say, 11:30?"

"Limo? Samantha, what the fuck is going on? What are you up to? This sounds mysterious and dangerous. I love it. See you at 11:30."

Samantha grinned. She loved tricking her friend, and the surprise she was about to deliver to Sophia would certainly surprise her.

She returned to Clive's office to say farewell. Clive immediately summoned Henry to drive her home or to her office. She explained she had arranged a luncheon with a friend. Clive enquired where. Samantha had not selected a restaurant. Clive called his Executive assistant and asked her to make a reservation for Samantha and a friend at 'La Bohème', and it was on the bank's account. Samantha could not believe her luck. 'La Bohéme' was one of the most popular and high-priced restaurants in the area. Getting a reservation was almost impossible and required planning months in advance.

Samantha said her farewells and left the bank feeling as if she were walking on a cloud. Henry was waiting for the elevator to escort her to the car. She gave him Sophia's address. He looked at it in surprise and smiled. She lived in the West Loop of Chicago, which was where 'La Bohème' was located, along with dozens of other fine restaurants and industrial buildings that over the last few years had been converted to expensive lofts.

"Your friend certainly lives in a nice and active area. Lots of art galleries and restaurants there. Maybe one day I could afford to live there. Now, that's a dream."

They stopped at an old 3-story brownstone building. The entrance had been modified to include a secure glass door with an electronic lock and surveillance cameras. The building oozed affluence.

Within minutes of their arrival, Sophia exited the building. Henry sprang from his seat with the speed of a sprinter to open the limo's rear door for her. Sophia smiled a disarming smile and purred a 'thank you' to him. Samantha had seen her seductive tricks before and smiled.

"OK, sister. What hole are we going to storm for lunch?"

"Well, I think for this occasion we will have lunch at 'La Bohéme'."

"What the hell is going on? A limo with a driver. One of the top restaurants in Chicago. You, a workaholic, are missing a day at the office. You owe me a big explanation."

"I will in good time. Over lunch."

Samantha glanced up and, in the car's mirror, observed Henry smiling at the scene.

"Miss Rose, what time should I return to pick you up after your lunch?"

Sophia looked at Samantha in bewilderment. Unsure of the situation, her bravado faded. They rode on to the restaurant in silence.

Upon arriving, Henry pulled into the private space at the curb and accompanied Samantha and Sophia into the restaurant. He spoke to the receptionist.

"Good morning. These are esteemed guests of The Communal National Bank. I believe there is a reservation."

"Yes, sir."

"Please call me at this number when our guests are ready to be picked up."

Henry could barely suppress a laugh as he turned to leave. He found the restaurant and its employees artificial and insufferable, but the food was magnificent.

The ladies were seated at a window table that looked out at the chaotic scene of Chicagoans fighting the snowy weather and hurrying about their business. Samantha felt secure and warm. She looked across the table at her friend and wondered how long she should keep her in suspense. She was enjoying teasing her.

"Sophia, tell me how your date with that handsome boxer went on Saturday night."

Sophia scowled and looked daggers at Samantha.

"Wouldn't you know it? He was fucking gay. What a waste of that fine physique."

Samantha laughed and decided it was time to unveil the secret.

"Sophia, we have been friends since high school. We have shared in each other's joys and agonies. I have a big decision to make. It won't be easy for me."

Sophia's face immediately showed concern. Anything that affected Samantha also affected her.

"What is it? You are behaving strangely. You are scaring me."

"It's Christmas. I don't know what to do. I have no date. I sort of have a loose plan to visit my mother, but my life has been disrupted, and I need to ask you something."

"Come on, girl. Stop talking in riddles. Spit it out. I know you. Stop playing with me."

Samantha had enjoyed keeping the suspense, but decided it was time.

"Sophia, before I tell you, let's get something strong to drink. I think you will need it."

She signaled an impeccably groomed waiter to the table. The Latino waiter arrived and patiently waited.

"Please bring us 2 large Vodka Gimlets. Be sure there are floating lime slices in the drinks."

"Of course, Madam."

After the waiter left, Samantha became serious.

"Sophia, what are you doing over Christmas and New Year?"

"Probably cleaning out my cat dish, doing laundry, and eating Christmas dinner at McDonald's. My family disowned me after I divorced Reverend Charles Villeneuve. They have decided that I am the evil one."

"Sophia, you never told me what happened. I know it was a messy divorce. Would it help you to talk to me about it?"

"Not really. Over the past 2 years, I have moved on, but it still stings. I loved that man and was prepared to do anything for him. He betrayed me big time. As a Reverend, I trusted and believed him. He was loved by our congregation."

"What happened? You two seemed so happy and in love."

" I had returned early to the house we owned then, and found him in our bed with 2 of his congregants providing a biblical anointment in a fashion that would make the most hardened porn star blush."

"I had no idea. I am sorry. You certainly didn't need that betrayal."

"In many ways, I am pleased as I have moved on and found skills and capabilities I never knew I had. Now, why don't you explain a thing or two about what is going on with you?"

"Sophia, I have won a great prize. It is a first-class, all-expense-paid trip to the Caribbean island of Aruba. It is for me and a companion, so you need to decide what to pack. I want you to be the one to come with me on a great vacation. We are both owed it after our crappy love lives."

"What? Where the hell is Aruba? Do they have food and electricity there?"

"Yes. It is a very popular vacation destination. After our lunch, we will return to my condo to research it. I have taken the day off work."

Sophia sat speechless, looking at Samantha. Finally, she spoke.

"Why me? Surely there is some handsome hunk you would want to go with."

"No. I think we will have great fun, and you are my bestie."

"When will we go?"

"We will decide this afternoon as we research the island. After lunch, we will go back to my condo and research this Aruba place."

Chapter 4

Making Plans

On an otherwise dreary day, their lunch became a session of frivolity. They joked about the things that had happened in their respective lives and how they had ended up at this stage of their lives.

The lunch was beyond comparison and enjoyed by both.

Samantha chose the Potato Vichyssoise and Smoked Bacon appetizer. Followed by the Spring Lamb with Green Asparagus and fresh Mint jelly. For dessert, she selected the Mango Soufflé with Rum and Shaved Coconut.

Sophia decided on a salad to start and picked the special of lettuce, cucumber, herbs, 5-year parmesan, and chardonnay vinaigrette. For her lunch, the choice was grilled tuna, haricot verts, tomato, potato, anchovy, olives and capers, quail egg, with a sherry vinaigrette. For dessert, Sophia chose a tart of prunes, candied walnuts, and served with vanilla ice cream made by the restaurant.

Over lunch, they consumed a large chilled bottle of Sancerre.

Samantha and Sophia were in a great mood and feeling no pain. Samantha looked at her watch. Lunch had taken over 2 hours. She was concerned and asked the waiter to contact Henry at the number he had left.

As they prepared to leave, the manager visited their table.

"Mr. Hutton just phoned. He wanted assurance that all had gone well with your lunch and time here. He is a very classy person."

The girls laughed, and Sophia gave Samantha a knowing look.

"Girl, I think you have attracted someone."

Before she could respond, Henry walked into the restaurant and beckoned them.

They drove to Samantha's condo in relative silence. Each was wrapped in the thought of a Caribbean vacation away from the cold and snow.

"Are you sure it is me you wish to share the prize with?"

"I need someone to chaperone me and keep me out of trouble, but honestly, I am not sure you are the right person for that."

"Me? I am so innocent, I should have been a nun."

For the rest of the trip, they bantered back and forth. Now and then, Henry would add some humor to the conversation. Outside, the weather continued to be foul and was deteriorating.

As they arrived at The Walden Towers, Henry turned to them.

"Miss Sophia, I am concerned that public transport will shut down if this keeps up. Mr. Jonas at the bank asked me to look after Samantha for the full day, so if you need to be driven home from her place, I will take you. Please contact me and allow some extra time for me to arrive and pick you up."

Henry then exited and opened the limo's rear door before escorting them inside.

In the condo, Samantha turned on the fire and fetched a bottle of cold Chablis and glasses. They sat at her dining table with her laptop and started their Aruba research.

Minutes became hours as they explored the various reviews on Facebook forums and the pictures users had posted. Both Samanatha and Sophia's excitement grew as they read and discovered the wealth of places to visit, things to do, and restaurants to try.

Hours passed by. They compiled a list of the attractions they felt would appeal to them the most. It was hard to decide, and often they engaged in friendly banter over the selection each had made. By the end of the bottle of Chablis, they had produced a lengthy list.

They were about to finish when Samanatha opened a Facebook post regarding the partying and fireworks associated with New Year's Eve. The post contained a video of the island lit up with fireworks at midnight.

Intrigued, Samantha searched for Aruba and New Year fireworks. She was rewarded with lots of posts and videos. For the next hour, she and Sophia opened and watched the videos.

"That's it. We are going to go for New Year's. Will that work for you, Sophia?"

"Yes, but you said you intended to spend Christmas break at your mother's."

"I will go and spend time before Christmas day and leave the day after. I will meet with Tracy from the bank's PR company tomorrow and see if we can travel on those dates. I hope your passport is up to date."

"If it's not, I will be at the passport office first thing in the morning."

"Do you think we will be able to find cruise wear and summer clothes in the stores at this time of year? I need a new bikini and some lightweight clothes. The temperatures in Aruba are very hot."

"Hmmmm. I know you, Samantha. You want new duds to catch some guy's attention. You've got plenty of summer wear. I've seen you in it."

Samantha laughed at her comment.

"I suspect you are speaking the thoughts of your own scheming."

Their revelry was interrupted by the ringing of Samantha's phone.

"Miss Samantha. This is Henry. The storm is getting worse. I suggest Miss Sophia leave now while we can still drive to her place, or she may want to consider staying with you overnight. We are in for a real dumper."

Samantha relayed Henry's concern to Sophia.

"No, I must go back to my place. Tell him to come immediately. I will be ready."

20 minutes later, Henry arrived to take Sophia to her home.

Morning arrived fast for Samantha. She jumped from her bed and stared from her living room window at the panoramic view of the park and river beyond. The storm had dumped so much snow that it had turned the Chicago area into a winter wonderland. The sky was bright blue. The sun beamed down on the sparkling crystals of snow. The few evergreen pine trees in the park had branches tipped with snow. The scene made Samantha happy.

She checked the time and made a decision. Wondering whether Tracy Brown was able to reach her office due to the weather, she decided to call her mobile phone. The phone was answered on the third ring. Samantha requested a meeting with her.

"Of course, but I suspect I will be a bit late getting to my office this morning. Yes, 10:30 will work for me. If I am late, there is a delightful little coffee shop on the ground floor of the building. They have the best pastries. Go there and wait. I will meet you there."

Samantha called her office.

Madge, the receptionist/administrator/coffee girl/do-it-everything girl, answered.

"Samantha, it's mayhem here this morning. Most of the partners are not coming in from their palatial abodes. Seems transit is down, and they don't want to drive. It's a zoo. Phones are ringing. Clients want to reschedule. Now, what can I do for you?"

"I have an appointment late this morning out of the office. I am working from home before I leave. I am wondering if you can get me the number for that client I need to cancel yesterday."

"Funny you should ask for that. The Mayor's office called. He wants you to call him about that case and set up a conference call with the city solicitor."

Samantha jotted down the number the Mayor's office had left for her to call back. Curious, she waited a few minutes and then called. To her surprise, Mayor Berg answered. Samantha introduced herself.

"Yes, thank you for calling back so soon. I need to arrange a conference call with Smidgen, the city solicitor handling this matter. Please hold."

Minutes ticked by.

"Samantha, I have Mr Smidgen with us. He will explain."

"Good morning, Miss Rose. We have spent considerable time and resources with the attorneys examining your case and the issue of conflict between the State and Municipal statutes regarding the matter. It is a complex legal dispute and has required careful navigation to evaluate and understand the implications of the competing governmental interests. Legal counsel advises us that there had been a similar case many years ago, and the court ruled that the City's bylaw was flawed. We have decided not to oppose your client's case. The City will be bringing forward a motion to modify the bylaw to align with the State law."

Samantha could barely suppress her glee.

"Thank you. That is great news for my client. Before I advise him, can I receive your decision in writing?

"Yes, I will try to have it to you by mid-January."

"I am wondering if you can draft a letter for me before then, as I am taking time to visit family and then a vacation over Christmas and New Year's. The matter is still scheduled for a court appearance this week, and we can both save money and the court's time by filing a resolution before then."

There was a silence until the Mayor spoke.

"I think that is an excellent recommendation. Mr. Smidgen, please draft a legal letter and have it delivered to Miss Rose this afternoon."

Samantha could barely believe her luck. This was the victory she needed to validate her professional skills and boost her confidence. She intended to show all the partners her success and especially boast about it to Terry Steele. She intended to dent his egotistical behavior. Her luck had changed over the past 24 hours.

Satisfied with how her day had started, she called for a taxi to take her to meet Tracy Brown.

She walked from her condo building out to the waiting taxi. Even though the sun shone brightly and the winds had dropped, the air felt cold and clean against her face. Samantha decided that, like the end of the storm, her recent days of stress and negativity were over. She decided the trip to Aruba was the start of a new chapter in her life.

Chapter 5

Final preparations

At precisely 10:30, Tracy Brown walked into the small coffee shop. Seeing Samantha, she waved and headed across to the table.

"Good morning. Wow, that was quite the storm last night. I guess you will be pleased to get away from this cold weather soon. Have you decided who will join you and the dates you wish to travel?"

Samantha proceeded to explain that she had decided to travel with her best friend and advised of the dates they wished to visit Aruba. Tracy frowned.

"That doesn't give me a lot of time to organize things, but I will do my best. I am sure it will be possible. It might be a little difficult as it is the peak of the high season in Aruba. Have you been able to research the island and select any activities?"

Samantha reached into her bag and pulled out the list she and Sophia had compiled. Tracy's eyebrows raised.

"That is certainly a complete list. May I take this as our company will need to contact some of these companies to make arrangements? I suspect we will not be able to make arrangements with some of the smaller ones, but I have this for you."

Tracy opened her attaché case and removed an envelope with the bank's logo on it. She handed it to Samantha.

"This is from Mr. Hutton. He understands you will need to pay for certain things while there. Since the prize is for an all-expense-paid trip, he insisted you take this."

Samantha opened the envelope and found that it contained a Platinum courtesy credit card inside. The card had a distinctive mother-of-pearl finish with the bank's logo embossed on it and Samantha's name. The card was protected in an RFI shielded, expensive, handcrafted leather wallet.

"Mr. Hutton has authorized a credit limit on this card for your use in Aruba. Now, back to the matter of the trip. I need you and your friend's passport info to make flight and travel bookings. Can you please arrange to send them to me as soon as possible?"

For the next hour, Samanatha and Tracy sat discussing Aruba and the planned trip, until Tracy needed to leave for an appointment at her office. Samantha glanced at the time and decided to take the rest of the day off. There was nothing urgent at her office. She would monitor her emails, and when the letter regarding the settlement of her client's case was received, she would contact him with the news. She dialled Sophia's number.

"Hi. I am going to visit a few stores and shop for some items for our trip. Care to join me?"

Sophia enthusiastically accepted the invitation and agreed to meet Samantha at the coffee shop.

After Sophia arrived, they plotted out the stores they wished to visit. Both were bubbling with excitement and looking forward to the trip ahead. Samatha quietly slid the credit card across the table while explaining who had arranged it for her.

"I tell you, girl. That boy has the hots for you. You'd better watch it or be prepared. Probably a better catch than that weasel, Terry Steele."

It was unlike Samantha to blush; however, Sophia's direct comment and tone caused her heart to skip, and she felt a slight embarrassment, but in her mind, she wondered.

"Don't be silly. It is all part of the prize, I am sure. Now let's get out of here and do some retail therapy."

The afternoon was a whirlwind of visits to Chicago's high-end fashion stores. Both Sophia and Samantha were giddy with the excitement of the upcoming trip. Swept up in their elated mood, they selected and tried on outlandish outfits and broke down, howling with laughter. The snobbish sales attendants were not amused and showed it.

By mid-afternoon, they had purchased new bikinis, summer dresses for the evening, capris, sandals, and a supply of cosmetics.

Samantha was eager to contact her client with the news from the Mayor's office.

"Sophia, I need to end this fun. I must return to my office. I have an important matter to attend to. I will call you later."

Samantha returned to her office in high spirits. Madge welcomed her.

"Samantha, thank God you are here. Today has been bedlam, and to make matters worse, your ex-flame, Terry Steele, is here and in a foul mood. He has been asking for you and demanding to know where you were. I have never seen him like that. If I were you, I would avoid him."

It was too late. Madge had no sooner finished speaking when Terry Steele arrived in the reception area. Samantha looked at him and took in his overall appearance. His face was flushed, and his normal, precise grooming was gone. His tie was twisted, and his shirt tails were partially untucked. It was obvious to Samantha that he had been drinking. She had seen it before.

Samantha picked up some papers from the reception desk and walked toward her office, attempting to ignore him. Calling her name, he stumbled after her. Samantha spun around.

"Terry Steele, for your own sake, I suggest you get out of the office immediately. If any of the other partners see you in that shape, your career at this firm is done."

"You bitch. If it wasn't for me, you wouldn't be here. Your legal aspirations would be dead."

Terry Steele attempted to reach out for her, but Samantha quickly stepped back, avoiding contact.

"Terry Steele, you are drunk. Go home before you do something stupid."

"I just want to talk with you. I never meant for those things to happen. I still love you. I need you. I am a wreck."

"You should have thought about that before you treated me like shit and belittled me in front of my friends and the partners here. No, Terry Steele, it's over. Get lost."

"Please sit with me and listen. I have some serious things to tell you."

Samantha thought back to the days she had spent with him when the relationship had been good. Instinctively, she knew something serious had happened. She decided that if it involved her in any way, she needed to find out.

"Come into my office. I am busy, but I will give you 5 minutes. I will ask Madge to monitor the situation. If you try anything funny, she will be instructed to call security or the police."

In her office, Terry Steele collapsed onto the sofa. Samantha pulled up a chair and sat across from him. She stayed silent. Terry Steele dropped his head into his hands and started sobbing. She maintained her calm and continued to sit, looking at him. She felt no sorrow for him.

Chapter 6

A vacation gift for Samantha

Samantha felt a growing frustration. She needed to contact her client, and Terry Steele's dismal behaviour was annoying her.

"If you have something to say, spit it out. I am busy and have a life that doesn't include you or your drama."

She observed that in his current state, his normally attractive features were gone. His good-looking, boyish face was drawn and tired. It was as if he had aged prematurely. She felt no pity for him.

"I am destroyed. I have made some serious errors. You remember the golf trip I made with my friends to the Bahamas."

"How could I forget that. You arrogantly put that ahead of our relationship, and I disliked the friends you were going with. I did not trust them."

"During our stay, I was introduced by them to some South American investors and property developers. They discussed a major project planned in Venezuela. It was a hotel, a shopping mall, and a Robert Trent Jones-designed golf course. Their project seemed solid. I had due diligence performed, and nothing negative was found. The financial administration was under the control of a company in the Cayman Islands. I was given a prospectus and offered an early investment position. I took it. To qualify for the early investor status, payment was required immediately. I was short and needed funds. I had just completed the merger transactions for the Pinnacle Plastics deal and had received payment into the trust account. I withdrew funds from the client account. I had planned on replacing the money within days. Even with the money, I was still short, so I needed to find additional funds. The bank turned down my loan request. I should have stopped then."

Samantha frowned and considered what he had told her.

"What you have done is illegal and stupid. However, if you replenish the client trust account immediately and there is no loss or damage, then the partners may elect to overlook your indiscretion."

"No, I don't think so. There is a lot more. During our relationship, when we were the best of friends, you and your mother had agreed for me to act as legal representative for the establishment of the Captain Owen Rose Estate trust accounts and investments. When the bank rejected my loan request, I directed several transfers of small amounts to the Cayman Islands bank for the developers. I transferred 3million. Your father's estate is large, and the investments continue to grow. I need you to officially lend me that amount and make the transfers legal."

"You stupid son of a bitch. I will do no such thing. Get out of my office now."

Slowly, Terry Steele rose and attempted to extend his arms to hug her.

"Samantha, I will repay you. Please set it up as a formal repayable advance. I can then provide the bank with the legal paperwork to proceed with the transfer."

"Get out, now."

Looking dejected and beaten, Terry Steele shuffled out of her office.

As she sat deciding on what actions to take, her laptop pinged as a new incoming email arrived. She checked and found a letter from Smidgen advising her and her client of the city's decision to withdraw the proceeding and approve her client's plan. Attached to the email was a scanned petition to the court withdrawing the action.

Samantha called her client and briefed him on the update. He was delighted. She informed him of her plan to be away from the office until mid-January, but would be checking her messages.

As she started to pack up her recent purchases to take home, her laptop pinged again. She looked at the email. It was from Tracy Brown confirming the flights they had requested. American Airlines First class, December 28th, direct from Chicago O'Hare to Aruba.

Tracy had attached the electronic tickets for both Sophia and Samantha. Also attached was a list of the different vendors on the island who would participate in providing services as part of the prize.

Samantha decided to review the email in more detail once she arrived home. The email improved her mood after Terry Steele's disgusting performance. She decided against taking the bus and called for an Uber.

Back in her condo, she called Sophia, and together they discussed the details of the trip. Samantha also brought up her confrontation with Terry Steele.

"Samantha, I suggest you call the bank in the morning. You must inform them in case he has some other devious plan. Do not trust him. You have time to address this before you leave for Christmas at your mother's."

Afterward, Samantha packed her vacation bag and made a call to 'Cattitude Cat Hotel' to arrange boarding for Horace, and to her mother to confirm the Christmas plans. She decided not to upset her mother with details of Terry Steele's actions. Her mother had never liked him.

When she had completed packing and arranging for her condo to be looked after in her absence, she sat with a glass of wine to gather her thoughts. She considered Sophia's advice to contact the bank regarding Terry Steele's attempt to access the trust accounts. She searched her purse for the business card Peter Hutton had given her. She dialled his direct number and left him a detailed message.

Her mind was running as she checked off the mental checklist of personal and business matters that required attention before she left on vacation. She was satisfied that everything was in order.

Her phone buzzed as a text message arrived. It was Sophia, and it read:

'Terry Steele has given you the best gift for Christmas and your vacation. He's finished. You are done with him. You won.'

Samantha smiled. Her friend always turned the bad into something lighthearted. She closed the lights and fire and left to prepare for bed.

Chapter 7

Last-minute details

It was early when Samantha's phone rang. She answered it to hear the voice of Peter Hutton wishing her a good morning.

"Samantha, I listened to your voicemail. I know you are probably rushing to get everything in order before you leave, but you must come to the bank. I need certain documents signed. Can you come soon?"

"Yes, I will be there at 10."

"I will see you then."

Samantha finalized her rental car reservation and finished tidying up some last-minute tasks at her condo before leaving for the meeting at the bank.

At the bank, she was welcomed and immediately escorted to Peter Hutton's office. She was surprised to find another man seated in the office.

"Samantha, let me introduce Fred Joyce. Fred is with the FBI Financial Crimes Unit. I have invited him here today to hear your story."

Fred nodded and greeted her. His expression was stern but kind.

"Please tell Fred the details regarding the transfers Terry Steele has attempted to execute."

Samantha told all she knew. She provided information on the reasons why Terry Steele had tried to access the trust funds. She disclosed his embezzlement of client trust funds at the law firm. Fred Joyce sat in silence.

Almost an hour passed before Samantha finished. Fred Joyce finally spoke.

"What you have told us is extremely serious. Our department is already aware of Mr Steele and his dealings. We have been working with Mr. Hutton and his Compliance Team for several months. His team alerted us to the circumstances surrounding the processes he tried to use to get the funds. He made several mistakes that triggered an investigation. In conjunction with Mr. Hutton, we allowed the bank to act as if the transfers were done, but advised Steele of a delay in processing times due to bureaucracy. He bought our explanations. We had also been contacted by the bank's regulators as they identified strange withdrawals from your firm's accounts that were signed for by Steele. Mr. Steele is about to be charged with Federal offenses, including fraud, money laundering, securities violations, theft, tax evasion, and participation in criminal gang activities related to illegal financial transactions. There are more."

"Samantha, if he is convicted, Mr Steele will be enjoying his time in a Federal penitentiary. Not a great place for a vacation. Yours will be much more enjoyable, I am sure. I ask that you keep all of this confidential. He will be arrested while you are on vacation. The authorities require time to assemble certain documents. Upon your return from vacation, we will require you to sign some statements regarding the trust. Thank you for coming this morning."

As she left his office, Clive Jonas called out to her.

"Samantha. Tracy has given me a copy of your plans. I see that you and your friend Sophia are leaving on the 28th. That American Airlines flight leaves at an ungodly early hour. I have requested

Henry to drive you and Sophia to the airport. It will be more convenient for you, plus you won't have the hassle of parking while you are gone. Henry will be in contact."

"That is very kind of you. I look forward to seeing you on my return and sharing my adventures in Aruba."

"Years ago, I went to Aruba on my honeymoon. My wife and I had a great time and visited the sister islands- Curacao and BonAire. Both are exceptional places to visit."

"I am so looking forward to this. There has been too much pressure in my life recently."

Part 2

Aruba happens

Chapter 8

On our way

Samantha returned from Christmas celebrations at her mother's. A few family relatives had joined them. All had been interested to learn about her upcoming trip to Aruba. She returned the rental car and completed packing some cosmetics and clothing for the trip.

The morning was still dark when Henry arrived to take them to the airport. She had taken her baggage to the lobby the night before, and Lionel, the concierge, had kept it safe for her. Henry took the baggage to the limo.

"Good morning, Miss Samantha. I'd better get you into the car fast since you are wearing summer clothes. Don't want you getting a chill. Is Miss Sophia ready for us?"

"Yes. I already called and made sure she was awake and waiting. I'm not sure she even went to bed."

Henry laughed and shook his head.

"Seems like you are both in high spirits for this trip. I am sure you will have fun and probably create some trouble. I wish I could come."

At that hour in the morning, the traffic was light. Henry made small talk over the soft jazz that was quietly playing. They had barely stopped outside Sophia's when she rushed out wearing a full summer outfit with large sunglasses perched atop her massive, brushed-up hair.

"Let's go, girl. I'm ready for some sun, relaxation, and a view of some fine bronzed male physiques."

Henry laughed and shook his head.

"I can see what sort of vacation you two will have. God help the single men trying to unwind there."

The trip to O'Hare was uneventful. Henry wheeled into the departures area for American Airlines, and after stopping, he signaled a luggage attendant to take the bags.

After checking in and clearing security, they made their way to the First Class lounge, where they were welcomed. The lounge was not busy. They selected private seats and watched as staff entered from the kitchen and replenished the breakfast foods laid out on a long table covered with a white starched cloth.

While seated, a waitress offered them the choice of juice, coffee, or champagne. Samantha decided to start her vacation with a mimosa. Sophia followed. With hours to wait until their flight boarded, they were in no hurry.

A tall man dressed in a full chef's uniform approached the breakfast bar, carrying a silver chafing dish, which he carefully placed at the center of the table.

Samantha observed wisps of steam arising from the dish. Curious about its contents, she walked over to the table and was delighted to find it contained freshly prepared Mediterranean Egg Scramble. She decided to spoil herself and spooned out a large serving, carefully selecting the ingredients of chopped spring onion, sliced cherry tomatoes, some black olives, and several pieces of finely diced bell peppers.

Sophia selected a version of Eggs Benedict and slathered Hollandaise sauce over the poached eggs.

After all, they proclaimed, "We are on vacation."

Gradually, the lounge started to fill up with the arrival of passengers in various modes of dress.

Samantha watched Sophia with amusement as she saw her examining the arrival of a group of businessmen. She realized at that moment that Sophia had a plan in mind for her vacation on the island. Samantha, however, had decided to use the time away from Chicago and the office to flush away the impact that Terry Steele had had on her life. The thought of an island vacation was the furthest thing from her mind. She was determined to just enjoy all the island could offer.

Time slipped by, and the receptionist at the greeting desk approached them and advised that the flight was ready for boarding.

They took the short walk to the gate and boarded the plane to occupy their first-class seats for the approximately 5-hour flight.

Within minutes, an extremely attractive Latino male flight attendant arrived with glasses of champagne.

"Good morning. My name is Hector, and I will be your servant for the flight, " he joked.

"Ladies, would you care for a glass of champagne to start your day and get you in the mood for your Aruba party? I assume you will party there."

"Well, Samantha, I'd certainly like to party with him."

Samantha and Sophia sat sipping the chilled champagne and watched as other less fortunate passengers filed through the cabin on their way to the economy seats.

With all the passengers seated, there was a slight jolt as the plane was pushed back from the gate. The cabin lights dimmed as the jet turbines were fired up and whined into life. Samantha looked at Sophia and smiled.

"We're finally on our way. Leaving behind all the BS of the office and Terry Steele. I'm putting my mind in vacation mode. To hell with everything."

Sophia raised her 3rd glass of champagne and toasted the comment.

They sank back into the seats as the plane accelerated down the runway and lifted into a climb for the 5-hour trip. Once the plane reached altitude, the Captain came onto the intercom.

"Welcome aboard our flight to the paradise of Aruba, where it is presently 83 and sunny with a stiff trade wind blowing from the east. We expect an uneventful and smooth flight today. Sit back and enjoy the ride."

Sophia's gaze was fixed on the flight attendant.

"Now that's something I'd like to ride and help pass the hours."

"Sophia, we haven't even left Chicago yet, and you are misbehaving. Oh God, what have I done, inviting you for this vacation? 10 days! I'm wondering if I'll survive them."

"Don't worry, sweetie. Just trying to get you to lighten up and forget the crap you are leaving behind. No Terry Steele, no legal infighting, no bitchy clients, so what could be better? Just 10 days with delightful me."

Samantha laughed and realized why Sophia had become her best friend. She was there in the best of times and the worst of times. She reached down and picked up her carry-on bag. She removed a slim folder and opened it.

"Sophia, let's go through this. It's a collection of the events and places that Tracy had put together for us. Some of them have been contacted by Tracy's company and will participate in providing services as part of the prize. Let's start with our arrival and where we are staying."

The flight attendant returned and poured a 4th glass of champagne for Sophia. She gushed a thank you, and from his expression, Samantha deduced more than just a passenger-airline employee level of interest.

From the folder, Samantha pulled a brochure describing their resort. The Bucuti and Tara resort located on Eagle Beach.

"Sophia, this resort sounds amazing. Look at these pictures and the description."

Interested, Sophia leaned across from her seat.

"We are being met at the Aruba Reina Beatrix airport and taken by VIP. Limo to the resort. It says here the resort has won many industry and traveler awards, and has been voted the number one resort in the Caribbean for the past few years. The resort has also won environmental awards. Sounds like a great place. Let's see what activities are there for us to enjoy."

Excitedly, they pored over the documents Terry had provided.

Hours slipped by as they giggled and imagined spending time in the spa. Lounging provocatively at the pool, enjoying the solitude of the white sands of Eagle Beach. Sophia's interest dwelt on the resort's restaurants. She read with keen interest some customer reviews on the Element's restaurant.

"Sammy, I wish I had a partner there so I could try dining under the private palapa on the beach. That gives me enough incentive to find one."

Their conversation was interrupted by the flight attendant asking which meal they wished to choose. After answering their questions, Samantha chose the Poblano Mexican-style chicken and rice with a diced fresh green and orange salad. Sophia hesitated and asked the attendant to repeat and describe the meals again.

"Yes, the Mexican chicken is served with herbed rice and a salad. The pasta is a meat-filled ravioli with a chunky tomato sauce. Both meals are served with a wine, a cheese selection, and bread buns."

Sophia gave the attendant a puzzled look before ordering the pasta and then mischievously asked.

"Do you have hot buns?"

The pun wasn't wasted on the attendant who cheekily relied.

"I can heat up my buns for you anytime."

Samantha shrank into her seat while attempting to suppress her laugh. She already knew what vacation lay ahead.

For the balance of the flight, they occupied themselves examining and deciding on activities contained in the various brochures that Tracy had provided.

Chapter 9

Aruba Arrival

When Samantha heard the noise of the plane's engines reduce and felt the plane tip as it circled, she woke Sophia from a light sleep that had been assisted by the many glasses of champagne.

"Sophia. Look out the window. There is Aruba."

From the front left-hand window, they stared out at the long white sands of Eagle Beach. As the plane dropped in altitude and approached the airport, they viewed cruise ships moored at the port of Oranjestad. Further inland, they could see the arid landscape and finally the hill, Hooiberg, before the plane touched down and bounced a little due to the high winds.

The sound in the cabin fell as the pilot cut the jets. They whined down to silence. Excited voices filled the void as couples and families chattered with the expectation of the days of adventure ahead.

Within minutes of the cabin crew opening the plane's door, warm, humid air filled the plane.

As first-class passengers, Samantha and Sophia were the first to be escorted off the plane. They breathed in the tropical air, thankful to be away from the cold, frigid temperatures of Chicago.

The walk from the gate to the arrivals hall was long and hot. Samantha was pleased she was not carrying any baggage. They walked down a flight of stairs and joined the queues of travelers from other flights waiting to clear Immigration and Customs. In less than a minute, they heard their names quietly called and turned to be greeted by a young man dressed in an impeccably tailored dark lightweight suit.

"Good morning and welcome to Aruba, ladies. I am Alberto, and I am your VIP Concierge. I will guide you through Immigration and Customs and assist with retrieving your checked baggage. Before we clear Customs, do you wish to shop at the airport duty-free for perfumes, wines, or anything?"

"No, it has been a long day so far, and we just want to reach the resort and relax."

"Ok then. As part of our service, you will be expedited through. There is no need for you to stand in those queues."

Alberto took their passports and the Aruban ED Card and went ahead to hand them to the Immigration officer. She looked at Samantha and Sophia before smiling and wishing them a great vacation.

A second man, pushing a luggage cart, joined Alberto, and he directed them all to the sleek black limousine waiting curbside.

Alberto opened the rear door and assisted them into the vehicle. A blast of cold air greeted them.

Sophia requested that it be reduced.

"I'm here for he tropical life. Don't need that. We left all that cold crap behind in Chicago."

"Miss Sophia, it's 42 degrees. You will cook."

"Alberto, that heat is what brings out my romantic tendencies."

Samantha looked to Alberto with exasperation.

"It's going to be a trip."

Alberto gave her a knowing smile.

"I see that you are staying at the Bucuti and Tara Resort. That is a beautiful upscale resort. You will be very pleased. Nothing but the best service, food, resort facilities, and the staff are beyond compare."

They pulled away from the airport terminal out to a large traffic roundabout encircled with high flagpoles displaying the flags of many different countries.

"Ladies, after we pass the airport perimeter, we will travel a short distance along the coast. If you are interested, I will point out some areas, unless you wish to travel in silence."

Sophia was the first to reply.

"No, please tell us, but first, what is that guy with the cart beneath the umbrella selling? I see there are some cars stopped there."

"Oh, he is a local and prepares fresh fruit drinks. Mango, coconut, Mispel, and more."

Samantha frowned.

"What is Mispel?"

"It is a dark green fruit similar in shape and size to an egg. It is ripe and ready to eat when it is almost about to decay. The taste is a combination of sweet and sour and can be compared to a sweet apple sauce. In some of the supermarkets here, you will see our local ice cream company has Mispel flavour they make."

"Please, can we stop? I would love to have a fresh fruit drink."

Alberto pulled across the busy road and stopped near the juice seller's stall. He slid from the driver's seat and opened the door for Samantha and Sophia, who immediately investigated the different fruits. Sophia was eager to try the Mispel. She listened as Alberto spoke rapidly to the man. She did not understand the language they were speaking and shrugged while gesturing to Samantha. Alberto turned to them.

"He does not have any Mispel here today. He suggests you visit him on Saturday at the local farmers' market, as he will have a fresh supply. At this time of the year, I recommend the fresh mango drink."

Samantha decided to pass on the drink, while Sophia was eager.

"I am curious. What language were you speaking with him?"

"Haha. He does not speak English. We were speaking Papiamento, the local language here."

"What is it like?"

Alberto smiled and described the various linguistic components of the language. Samantha was fascinated and decided to buy a book and learn more, and try to learn some Papiamento.

With a drink in hand, they continued the drive. Alberto pointed out various locations. To their left, the turquoise waters of the Caribbean met the bright white sands of a long beach. Alberto pointed out Governors Bay, and a little further on, he told them a story of the area called Pardenbaii. He told them of long past days when ships would stop in the little natural harbor and release horses that would transport cargo through the shallow waters. He advised them to look for the blue horses as they passed into Oranjestad, and gave a brief story about the horses.

Samantha commented on all the festive decorations on trees and lampposts along the road and on the large nativity display outside the Aruban Parliament.

"Yes, we love our Christmas. Aruba is primarily a Catholic island, and it is one of the happiest religious times of the year for us."

As they arrived at a small bridge crossing a canal, the traffic slowed to a crawl. On the left, Samantha looked in awe at 3 large passenger cruise ships docked.

"It's a busy day in our port today. The traffic is always slow when the ships are in. The tourist passengers walk around the stores for souvenirs, and there is congestion as they cross the street. Each of those ships brings in over 3000 passengers. " They crawled along through Oranjestad. Samantha admired some of the old Dutch architecture and decided a walking visit was in order.

They rode on until they reached another roundabout with a large sculptured Conch shell in the center. Alberto turned left off the main road, drove down a narrow street, and turned right to the Bucuti and Tara Resort. A seated security guard raised a barrier, and they continued to the resort entrance.

Alberto slowed to a halt, and as he did, a young man in a casual uniform emerged from the entranceway carrying a tablet. He opened the door before Alberto could leave the driver's seat.

"Miss Samantha and Miss Sophia, welcome to Aruba and the Bucuti and Tara Resort. My name is John, and it is my pleasure to introduce you to the resort and answer any questions. You don't need to register, as it has all been handled. Instead, would you like a cold, fresh, moist towel to freshen up from your trip and maybe enjoy a glass of complimentary champagne or a cool beverage?"

They declined the drinks, and John arranged for their baggage to be delivered to their rooms before walking with them through the resort's grounds.

The immaculate tropical gardens impressed Samantha. John continued with the tour, pointing out the gym, the spa, the inside restaurant, and describing the Elements restaurant for dining outside and on the beach. Sophia drooled at the thought of a romantic evening dinner on the beach under the large private palapa.

"Miss Samantha, you will be staying in the penthouse suite of the Tara, and Miss Sophia, you will have a gracious private room of your own."

They rode an elevator, which Samantha considered the quietest she had ever been on, to the penthouse floor.

Upon reaching the penthouse, John opened the door. They entered into the beautifully appointed suite and were struck by the huge sliding glass door with the expansive view of the Caribbean Sea. John opened the door, and they walked out onto a small balcony and stood for several minutes absorbing the view of the white sands of Eagle Beach below them and the blue of the sea, while a cooling breeze refreshed them.

After a few minutes, John took them inside to show the bedroom and a fully equipped kitchen. Samantha was ecstatic.

The bedroom had the same panoramic view. She would be able to lie in bed and view the bright blue sky and the ocean.

"I will now take Miss Sophia to her suite. Your bags should arrive any minute. I will leave you now, but if there is anything you need or have any questions, I will be at the main concierge desk."

Tired but happy, Samantha kicked off her shoes and returned to the balcony to rest.

"This is paradise," she thought, before drifting into a light sleep.

Chapter 10

Samantha was awakened by the continuous loud knocking at the door to her suite. Grogily, she went to the door and opened it to find Sophia there, dressed for the beach. She took in Sophia's beach attire and shook her head.

Sophia had changed into the skimpiest, almost nude, skin-toned pink bikini that was still visible through the light wrap she wore. She wore a large floppy white hat with her curls poking out from under the brim. Sophia picked up on her reaction.

"Hey girl, at our age, if we still have it, then I say use it before it fades."

Samantha couldn't help but laugh. Sophia always had a well-intentioned comeback for most things.

"Give me a minute to change, though I doubt I will be any competition for you."

Minutes later, Samantha emerged from her room wearing a startling white and red one-piece bathing suit and carrying a matching cover-up. On her head, she wore a pink baseball cap with her hair pulled back in a ponytail and pushed through the slot at the back of the hat.

"I want to stop at the concierge desk on our way out to the beach to ask about activities."

"Yes. That is an excellent idea."

They found John seated and speaking on the phone. He gestured to them to sit across from his desk. He finished his conversation and turned his attention to them.

"Is everything fine with your suites? Is there anything you need?"

"Everything is better than fantastic. I want to use our time to explore and enjoy some activities here on the island. What do you recommend? I would like to start with a tour of the island to see the unique points of interest and learn about its history."

John sat back with his hand cradling his chin while he thought.

"Do you wish to be part of a tour group or a private tour?"

"What do you recommend?"

"There are several large tour operators on the island. They have established routes and drive from one location to another. They stop for brief periods to allow the tourists to leave the buses for pictures and to see things close up. The groups are often large, and if you want to spend a little more time at any of the locations, it is generally not possible, as they have fixed schedules and operate at pre-established, tight times. There are several small, intimate private operators as well. They are often more flexible and offer narratives describing the island and any history related to the locations."

"I think my preference would be a more intimate tour."

John sat thinking for a minute before responding.

"There is a possible issue we may encounter. It is the Christmas and New Year's time. Most activities are fully booked, or the operators and staff are booked off for the holidays. There is one operator I can contact who offers a very personal service. He takes people to locations on the island that most of the larger operators visit, but also will show you places that many don't even know exist. He will make the day an experience and customize the tour. Should I contact him?"

Samantha turned to Sophia and asked her opinion.

"Yes. I am wondering how intimate though. Sounds like it could get exciting."

"Sophia, behave."

John laughed as he punched numbers into his phone.

"This operator is small and not associated with our resort. At this time of year, he may be with family and not working."

John held on as the phone continued ringing unanswered. He finally hung up, looked at Samantha, and shrugged.

As he turned away to consult with an associate, his phone chirped. It was a return call from Alex of Dushi Tera Experience. John explained Samantha's request and then listened while Alex responded. John held the phone away and explained.

"Ladies, he is about to start Christmas celebrations and will be closing. He has a cancellation for tomorrow, but after that, he will not be available until early January. Do you wish to book?"

Samantha nodded, and John handed her the phone to make the arrangements.

"Well, that's arranged. He will pick us up here at 8:30 tomorrow morning. John, you have concerned me about the island being busy. There are some things I would like to book. Can you assist?"

"Certainly. That is why we are here. To make things as pleasant and as stress-free as possible. What would you like to book?"

"I love the water and want a fun cruise, but not too crowded."

"Do you want to go on a morning, afternoon, or sunset cruise?"

John reached across his desk and handed Samantha a brochure for the Jolly Pirate Cruise.

"This is always fun. They have an early morning sail, which is a little more reserved than the later ones where people enjoy a few drinks, and some more than a few."

"This looks perfect. Can you please get us booked the day after tomorrow?"

John wrote down the information. As Samantha and Sophia left for a late lunch at 'Elements' on the beach, he advised them to stop at the desk after lunch for the details.

They strolled to the restaurant and selected a shaded table.

"This sure beats fighting the crowds in Chicago. I love this resort. It's better than I had hoped."

A waitress arrived at their table and offered drinks. It didn't take Sophia long to order.

" I think I should try one of those Aruba Aribas I hear about."

"And I would like a chilled Chablis, please."

The drinks arrived, and they sat reading through the lunch menu while enjoying them.

Samantha put down her glass.

"I am feeling a little tired, so I will just have a light lunch. I will take the Moroccan Eggplant. How is it prepared?"

" Madam, it is twice-baked, rubbed with Moroccan spice, drizzled with grapefruit, crumbled feta cheese, a homemade dressing, and tortilla chips crumble. It is served chilled."

Sophia pondered the menu and finally unleashed her desire.

"I'm hungry, so those Jerk Chicken Tacos sound good, and please, bring a bottle of the Aruban Chill beer. Are those tacos good?"

"The order is comprised of marinated chicken strips, black bean, melon and pineapple salsa, crispy onion rings, and homemade jerk chicken sauce. They are served with guacamole and sour cream. There is a Gluten-free option available if you need. I am sure you will enjoy them."

After lunch, they strolled along the white sands of Eagle Beach before it was too hot, and then they headed to the resort's pool.

Samantha lounged after soaking in the pool. She was happy.

"I am so pleased that it is so subdued and relaxing here. This is what I need after all the drama with Terry Steele and the pressures at the office. Thank goodness no children are playing that loud and annoying Marco Polo game. I appreciate the quiet."

"Girl, you are no fun. I think a little male companionship is what you require to get you refocused on life. Forget Terry Steele. He is going to be handled by the authorities. Just treat him and what he did, as you would when prosecuting any other case."

"My mind is far from Terry Steele. I am concerned, however, that whatever financial shenanigans he played have not damaged the trust accounts. I worry that my mother's investments are safe."

"You are a good daughter. You care about her so much, but now it's time for you to let your hair down a bit and live."

Their conversation was interrupted by John, the concierge.

"Ladies, I need to advise you concerning booking the activities for you. Alex of Dushi Tera is available tomorrow. He can pick you up at the resort at 8:30 for a 4-hour or all-day trip. I spoke to Carla at Jolly Pirates, and she can confirm you on the morning sail, the morning after tomorrow. Should I confirm both bookings? It is the high season, and the demand is high. If you can let me know soon. The trips will soon be booked out."

Sophia answered for them both.

"No need to delay. Yes, please confirm for us."

"Will you ladies be requiring dinner reservations at any of the fine restaurants on the island?"

"No, after traveling today, I think we will stay here. Is it possible to book that private palapa on he beach?"

"I will check, but at this time of year, it is difficult. Do you have flexibility with the time you wish to dine?"

"Yes, we are flexible."

Sophia pouted an insincere face and commented.

"But not too late. I will want to dine amongst all the handsome hombres here."

Again, Samantha shook her head and leaned back to continue her sunbathing.

"Ladies, I strongly suggest you visit the store and buy some sunscreen protection. The sun is very strong in Aruba. The constant winds disguise the burning, and many find out too late."

Samantha thanked him and rose to visit the store.

They spent the afternoon poolside chatting and resting. Samantha's tranquility was occasionally interrupted by Sophia's running commentary, which provided a detailed rating on the physical attributes of certain members of the opposite race. She could not help but laugh at some of the ludicrous descriptions that only Sophia could devise.

The afternoon was slipping toward the end of the day. Samantha decided to return to her room and invited Sophia to join her on the balcony to watch the amazing golden sunset for which she understood Aruba was famous.

On returning to the penthouse, she found a folder containing the confirmation for the Dushi Tera trip and a map of Aruba showing the areas of interest. There was also a confirmation for an 8:00 pm dinner reservation in the private beach palapa.

Ecstatic, yet tired from the afternoon of swimming, sunning, and boy watching, they arranged their chairs in the most favorable location to view the sunset.

After the sun had set, Sophia left to prepare herself for dinner. Samantha was pleased to have some time alone. She was tempted to lie down, but was afraid she might drift off into a sleep and miss dinner. She idly flipped on the room TV and scanned the news before turning it off to avoid the deluge of bad news from an evil world intruding into her relaxed and happy state of mind.

Dusk faded into the darkness of night. In the private palapa, Samantha and Sophia examined the Elements Dinner menu. Samantha chose the Ginger Mahi-Mahi, a seared mahi, prepared and served in chardonnay and ginger cream sauce. Sophia selected the Chateaubriand, a tender beef tenderloin, served with béarnaise sauce and white asparagus.

A soft, gentle breeze blew through the palapa, and they sat quietly listening to the waves breaking at the shore. The sky was a deep purple-black, clear and without the city lights, and the stars shone like bright jewels.

Tiredness closed in quickly on them, and they decided to take an early night and be prepared for their trip with Alex and Dushi Tera in the morning.

Chapter 11

The Dushi Tera Experience.

Samantha and Sophia, dressed appropriately in shorts and tropical tops, with new running shoes, waited in the lobby area. It didn't take long before a large jeep with Dushi Tera Experience emblazoned on the side pulled into the reception parking area.

Sophia gasped loudly as she observed a tall, bearded man wearing fashionable sunglasses and dressed in khaki shorts and a form-hugging casual shirt jump from the jeep and head toward them.

"Bon Dia , Samantha. I am Alexander with Dushi Tera Experience. I am pleased to meet you both.

 I'm going to explain to you a little bit about how my tours are set up and what we will be doing, or what I would recommend for us to do.

Basically, I have customized a tour for you and your friend. We're going to do the highlights of what I believe to be the nicest spots on the island, and also a few secluded spots. Most, if not all, tour groups will not go to them. The Experience is worth every penny."

Alex laughed,

" So, no one's ever asked me to disclose the names to them because I just simply won't. We will do the park, the Arikok National Park. Inside the park, we have, obviously, the famed Conchi, which is also known as a natural pool. So we will be going there. That requires an off-road drive to it. It's a pretty rough drive. It takes anywhere from twenty to thirty minutes, depending on where we stop, if we stop along the way.

Once we get to the natural pool, I'll explain all the details as far as safety goes, and we will see whether the pool is open or not, because the pool is not always open. If the ocean is rough, we close the pool down for safety purposes. But it looks like the weather is good, so hopefully the pool will be open. And, I provide snorkel gear. There's good snorkeling inside the pool. There's a lot of fish in there, and so it's definitely worth taking a snorkel.

After the natural pool, we have to go off-road back to the main entrance of the park. But before we get to the main entrance, we would stop at a place we call Moro, and it's more of a place to look at. It's Moro, spelled m o r o. The nickname for Moro is also little Aruba, and that's because there is a little island that looks like Aruba. It's the leftover cliff that the waves didn't cut out.

After we pass by Morro, we're going to go back to the main entrance. We will pass the main entrance and head towards a beach we call Dos Playa. That beach, for me, has a history because we used to go and play in the water there and surf. Although there are signs that say that you shouldn't swim there, those signs are there primarily because we process so many tourists every year. And, we don't want people to go swimming there because of the undercurrents, the riptides, etc. So surfing is allowed, and, you know, you might see a local swim there, but it's not in it's not encouraged to swim there. No one's encouraged to swim there.

We will then head to Dos Playa, pass by Boca Prince, and then go to Fontaine Cave. The Fontaine Cave is fairly nice. It's small, but it has Indian drawings in there, and that's what makes it interesting. The Indian drawings are anywhere from five hundred to a thousand years old.

Next to that cave, we have a place we call the fish pedicure pond. And this is where people like to stick their feet in the water and have these fish, that are Amazonian cichlids, nibble on their toes, on their feet. What the fish are doing is removing dead skin.

Once we leave Fontaine Cave, we will then go to a cave we call Quadirikiri. It is a far bigger cave. It's got a pretty good bat population. It's nice for picture taking. I call that the picturesque cave. Fontaine Cave is more of a historical cave because of the drawings in there.

So once we get done with Quadirikiri Cave, we will exit the park, and we will head towards Baby Beach. On the way to Baby Beach, we will find a natural bridge that is the most beautiful natural bridge on the island, in my opinion. It does not get a lot of tourists, so I am sure it'll be of interest.

If you want, we can hike down to the bridge and take some pictures. It makes for really beautiful pictures. And, if you're willing, I will be more than happy to guide you down there and take beautiful pictures with you and Sophia. Once we're done with the natural bridge, we will drive by the pet cemetery, or more better said, the dog cemetery, on the way to Baby Beach. And then I'll show you Baby Beach and Rogers Beach.

From there, we will head towards what is known as Blackstone Beach. By Blackstone Beach, there's the Tripod Bridge. That's a bridge, that is one bridge, with three arches. So, it's almost like a spider looking like with the center and then three arches off the center. And that too is right next to a beach we call Andicuri Beach, a very popular beach, although it does not get a lot of visitors except for the UTV crowd. It is a beach we used to play at as kids, and also surf and swim out there.

Then there is another place that I consider a secluded, area, that we will take that I will take you to. There is a little pool in the rocks. I call it a rock pool. It's very unknown.

I take my guests there. You have to be fit to go there. You have to be able to climb a few rocks and crawl over a few things, but it's worth it, one hundred percent worth it. Super romantic if you want it to be. And so, it's a beautiful place to take some nice pictures, also.

That, in a nutshell, ladies, will be our tour. It'll probably take anywhere from six to seven hours, so it'll be an all-day tour. You can set the pace of your tour. I don't time any of my stops. So if you're enjoying your time at the natural pool, for example, and you wanna stay there for an hour, no problem. You wanna stay there for two hours, not a problem. It's your time. It's your money, so we do what you want. There is another special stop I sometimes make if you are interested. I can show you where I live because I live in a traditional Aruba home, which is called the Cunuku House. I bring some guests there who are interested, just to show them what it was like in the past. They don't build these types of homes anymore unless people want the same old look, but they're usually modernized. But I live in a traditional one, so we can make that a point of interest, to stop at.

Alright. So I hope this works for you."

Samantha and Sophia were overwhelmed.

"Hold a minute or two. That sounds like a busy day. I think I need to go pee before we leave."

Alex continued laughing as he watched Sophia head across the lobby at speed.

"Alex, she is a good person, kind and funny. You will get used to her."

Alex placed a small step stool at the front door of the Jeep and assisted Samantha up and into the cabin. He repeated the process for Sophia upon her return and settled her into the back seat.

"Do you ladies have everything you need? Cameras, sunscreen, water?"

Minutes later, the jeep lurched forward, and they were on their way to an unforgettable adventure.

The jeep accelerated away from the resort and along Eagle Beach before Alex turned inland. They drove past Tanki Leendert and eventually arrived at Brights Bakery, where Alex stopped.

"Let's go inside. I'm sure you will find something to tempt you. I will pick up some juices and water for our trip."

Alex selected a beef pastechi, while Samantha and Sophia chose some cashew cake and cinnamon buns. They were curious about the pastechi and asked Alex about it.

"A pastechi is a crescent-shaped Aruban pastry similar to an empanada. Unlike the empanada, the pastechi is made with a sweet, flaky pastry. The empanada is made with a heavier corn dough. Our pastechis are deep-fried and are filled with seasoned beef or cheese, ham, or vegetables. They are a common breakfast item."

Samantha was intrigued and selected a beef-filled one. Sophia was unable to pass on selecting a fresh whipped cream-filled pastry horn. Alex and Samantha laughed as Sophia demolished the treat and decorated her face with icing sugar and flecks of cream.

They continued their drive until they reached Santa Cruz and a sign directing them to Arikok Park.

After driving a little while longer, they dropped down an incline and arrived at 2 buildings at the entrance into the park. Alex stopped, and they entered the buildings where there were displays and descriptions of the wildlife found in the park and information on the history and features of the park.

After purchasing their passes, they continued driving. Alex took a branch in the road to the left. Within a couple of hundred yards, the sealed surface of the road turned into a caked dirt track. The jeep swayed side to side and bucked as each rocky bump jolted through the cab. The further in they drove, the more remote and rugged the track became. Alex slowed at times, as well as stopping to show them certain plants and flowering cacti.

Samantha felt her anxiety grow as the track narrowed and each side of the red soil and rocky track fell away precariously, with drops ranging from a few feet to deep, rugged rocks and cactus below.

Alex engaged the 4-wheel drive and cautiously climbed to a high point. He stopped, and they all climbed out of the jeep and looked down to see Oranjestad, Eagle Beach, and the hotel strip off in the distance. It was an amazing view.

The further they drove, the rougher the drive became. Alex bounced the jeep over an area of volcanic rock and stopped. Agia, they got out of the jeep, fighting against the strong winds buffeting in from the ocean and up the barren cliffs. They walked to the edge and viewed the Natural Bridge.

Back in the jeep, they continued onto the Conchi or Natural Pool. Sophia bounded from the jeep, determined to descend the stairs down to the pool. Samantha mustered up the courage and, with Alex's assistance, gingerly made her way down to the pool.

Waves crashed against an opening and seawater cascaded into the pool. Sophia climbed the rocks to jump into the pool. She was assisted by one of the park rangers. Samantha took a more refined plunge into the waters.

After 30 minutes. Alex called them from the pool, and wet and happy, they climbed back up the stairs to the jeep.

Before continuing, they all drank water and juice. Alex continued the drive until they reached the entrance to the Fontein cave.

"Let's go inside. I will take my black light, and you will be able to see the old Indian drawings. I will explain some of them to you, but there are many that are not understood. Unfortunately, there has been vandalism and some graffiti painted on them. I will show you the difference between the real and fake drawings."

Inside the cave, Alex shone his black light at the ceiling. Centuries-old drawings displayed in ochre, with dark lines depicting the shape of the object. Large dark cockroaches darted away from Alex's light.

Further in the cave, Ales pointed out the stalactites hanging from the ceiling of the cave and explained the colorization that had occurred over many years as rainwater seeped through the ground and brought mineral traces into the cave, and ran down and through the stalactites. They walked deeper into the caves, navigating their way around the stalagmites that poked up from the ground.

Alex shone his light into the entrance of a smaller cave within the main cave. Several bats hung sleeping. As he swept his light across the cave, he caught a large scorpion in the beam. It scurried into a crack. That was enough for Samantha, who wished to make a hasty retreat from the musty, earth-smelling cave.

Back in the bright daylight, they sat in the cool air conditioning of the jeep and chatted about what they had seen in the cave. Alex then started the jeep and drove to the Quadirikiri cave. It was larger than the Fontaine cave and required them to climb some steep stairs to enter the cavernous cave. For the next 15 minutes, they explored the cave.

With the adventuring of the Arikok park done, they then drove out through the park to Rogers Beach, where Samantha and Sophia swam and relaxed.

After spending time at Rogers Beach, Alex decided to drive them back to their resort, but show them more items of interest. He drove them past a very crowded Baby Beach and a little further along the coast, pointed to an area immediately adjacent to the water.

"That, ladies, is Pet Cemetery. All those crosses you see mark the graves of locals' loved pets who have passed on."

Both Samantha and |Sophia were moved.

Alex continued to drive, and they ascended a small mountain. At the top, Alex showed them the remains of the gun placements that had been installed and manned by the US during World War II. The vista encompassed unobstructed views of the east, south, and west coasts of the island.

Finally, Alex commenced the drive back to the Bucuti and Tara Resort.

Tired and happy, Samantha and \ Sophia thanked him and retired to their respective rooms to freshen up and relax for the evening ahead.

Chapter 12

Night out

After the action they had experienced on the Dushi Experience, neither Samantha nor Sophia felt like retiring for the night. However, at the recommendation of Alex, they visited one of the famous food trucks and ordered some 'street food'.

The food was plentiful and delicious. Based on Alex's advice, Samantha ordered a *patacone,* a fried plantain skin with a rich pink sauce. Her curiosity was satisfied when the street vendor handed it to her, accompanied by a dish of fried flaky white fish. Sophia elected a cheese and ham-filled *pastechi*, an Aruban favorite. The pastechi was hot, and the cheese and ham filling oozed from the flaky, crescent-shaped pastry.

They wandered through the Palm Beach Highrise Hotel strip, stopping to look at items offered for sale at the little kiosks. Samantha found a miniature ceramic turtle with a humorous expression on its face.

"That will sit on my desk to remind me of this trip. Better that than the picture I had of Terry Steele."

At the mention of his name, Sophia scolded her.

"I told you to forget him and enjoy this trip. I saw the way that Alex was watching you. I suspect he has more than just a fleeting interest in you. Hey girl, could this be the start of a holiday romance?"

Sophia laughed and ducked to avoid the friendly punch from Samantha.

The strip was busy with tourists from different nationalities browsing the stores and frequenting the many restaurants. There was the constant hum of conversations, punctuated by laughter and the occasional loud burst of a foreign language.

After Chicago and the constraints of her position as a lawyer, Samantha found the atmosphere exhilarating. It was lively and had a distinctly friendly feel.

As they continued walking, the sounds of live music and lively chatter from a piano bar named Sopranos attracted them. Always ready for some action, Sophia dragged Samantha into the crowded bar. The ambiance was that of a lively group. Reduced lighting contributed to the bar's appeal. Waitresses carrying large trays of drinks worked the crowd. Several couples danced on a small, makeshift dance floor. Badly sung strains of Rod Stewart's 'Sailing' met with mixed reaction from the crowd. Overall, the mood was positive, and surprisingly, Samantha found herself enjoying the place. In Chicago, she rarely visited nightclubs or bars. She justified her present enjoyment as an event unique to her vacation.

Sophia gently tapped her on the arm and asked Samantha to mind her purse while she left to dance. While Sophia danced, Samantha looked around at the crowd and observed an attractive fortyish man who had been watching her since they arrived at the bar. He raised his hand and gave her a small wave, and flashed a brilliant white smile at her. She shrank in embarrassment.

The volume of the music increased. When Sophia returned, Samantha wished to leave. Sophia questioned her why when the night was young.

"It is too soon after Terry Steele and that terrible relationship for me to become involved with anyone, let alone a vacation one-night romance. I want to leave."

"You need to get over it and move on. He looks nice, and from his appearance, I suspect maybe there is some wealth there."

"Sophia, stop it. Besides, I don't want to stay out too late. We have to be at Jolly Pirates early in the morning."

"I swear that at times you are no fun."

As they were preparing to leave, the man stood and walked away from the booth he was sharing with others and headed straight to Samantha.

The tall, tanned Latino with dark, expressive eyes, grey flecked hair, and a statuesque physique reached out his hand to her.

"Hi. My name is Sebastiano Peña. I have been watching such a lovely apparition since you walked in. I would love to share a dance with you."

Samantha blushed and stammered as she attempted to speak. Sophia laughed at her.

" I am sorry, but we are just leaving. Maybe another time."

"Yes, maybe tomorrow night then. I am staying just across the road at the Hyatt Hotel. Do we have a date to dance tomorrow night?"

Sophia took control.

"My friend, Samantha, and I will be here. She will be delighted to join you for a dance."

"Good, then it is settled. I look forward to tomorrow night. Bon Noche, Samantha."

Outside, Samantha was furious with Sophia.

"Why did you give him my name? How do you know I will return to Sopranos tomorrow night? He certainly looks nice, but as you know, those men who look like store mannequins or models are generally riddled with problems and baggage. I will find my partner in good time. Please don't do that again. I know you meant no harm, but I need space right now."

They strolled away from the bar and at an ice cream store, bought two cones and sat out on a bench, people watching.

"Let's take a taxi and go back to the Bucuti. I am tired." Sophia shrugged and agreed.

At the Bucuti, Samantha relaxed and apologized to Sophia.

"I did not drink at the bar and had nothing all night, so what say you and I go up and out on the balcony for a nightcap before we sleep in advance of our Jolly Pirates trip? I am not angry with you. It is something I need to get over."

"But, Samantha. That was one hunk of a man."

"Sophia, stop it."

On the balcony, they sat, watching the reflection of the moon on the Caribbean while sipping on their Baileys.

After an hour, they decided the night was over and agreed on meeting in he morning ahead of the Jolly Pirates trip.

Chapter 13

Jolly Pirates Sail

At 7:00 am, they left the Bucuti in a taxi for Moomba Beach and the Hadacurari dock, where the Jolly Pirate kiosk was located and passengers gathered.

The kiosk did not open until 8:30, but Samantha decided to stroll the dock and speak with the fishermen returning with their early morning catches.

The fishermen were unloading mahi-mahi, wahoo, barracuda, snapper, and other species that neither she nor Sophia knew. At 8:00, they went to the Hadicurari restaurant for early morning coffee.

Monica Jean, the bubbly and happy restaurant supervisor, had just opened up and welcomed them. They ordered two cappuccinos and watched as other passengers for the sail arrived at the kiosk.

Samantha gasped and grabbed Sophia's wrist while pointing across to the kiosk. Standing dressed in smart tropical casual wear was Sebastiano.

"I want to cancel. I am not going. This is a disaster."

She looked across at him and scanned to see who he was with. In particular, her radar was searching for the presence of an accompanying lady. He was with another man carrying snorkel equipment, but there was no sign of any female accompaniment. She was in no mood for a petty competition.

"You are going. You are meant to be the fearless lawyer who dominates in the courtroom. Get yourself together. He is just a person. Make the most of it. You need some friends."

They paid Monica and sauntered across to the kiosk. After checking in, they joined other passengers in walking down the dock to the waiting shuttle boat that would ferry them out to the replica pirate ship.

On the dock, the crew of the boat assisted passengers down and onto the ferry. The sea was calm, and the short few-minute ride from the dock out to the boat was smooth. When they reached the boat, passengers scrambled to get from the ferry and find a favorite position for the sail. Samantha and Sophia were among the last to exit.

Samantha looked up at the hand extended down to assist her. It was not a crew member, but the hand of a smiling Sebastiano. She clasped his hand and was surprised by how soft it was. She hesitated for a moment, then, as she started to climb out, Sophia gave her a strong push in her rear while laughing.

"Sebastiano, thank you. I am surprised to see you here."

"My friend here wants to snorkel over the wreck of that old wartime German ship, the Antilla."

"My friend, Sophia, wants the same. I don't know where she gets all her energy. There are times I can't keep up with her."

With all the passengers aboard, the crew assembled everyone for a safety announcement, followed by a description of the planned sail.

A member of the crew ran forward and released the boat from its mooring. Other members worked on unfurling a sail and partially raising it. The boat's engine sputtered into life and powered the boat around so it pointed north. They started to cruise out under power, and eventually, the engine was shut down.

Many of the passengers retreated inside under the cover of the rear cabin. Samantha found a place on the deck and sat admiring the coastline as they cruised along. It wasn't long before the crew announced that complimentary drinks were being served. Samantha decided to pass. Sophia joined her on deck, carrying a yellow drink.

"Don't worry. It's a weak mimosa. I won't drink too much as I want to swim out over the wreck."

Sebastiano arrived beside them and offered to bring Samantha a drink or coffee. She declined, and he left to find his friend. Sophia scowled at her.

"Damn it, Samantha. He was just being pleasant. What is wrong with you? This is a great opportunity to meet people from different countries and cultures. Take advantage. Soon we will be back in tight-assed Chicago with all the wannabes and game-playing fakes. Loosen up."

"You don't understand. It's not that I don't want to get to know him, it's because I am scared and feel inferior about meeting a man after what happened."

"Oh, what perfect BS, and coming from you. Either you get out of that shell, or I will do it for you."

Time slipped by as they cruised until an announcement over the PA informed everyone they had arrived at the Antilla, and soon it would be possible to pick up snorkels and fins from a crew member and go overboard to explore the wreck. Fortunately, the weather had cooperated, and the waters around the wreck were calm and smooth.

After the announcement, another member of the crew gave a brief history of the ship.

"Ladies and Gentlemen. There is an interesting story about the Antilla. It was a new ship that had just been launched in Germany just before World War II. The ship, the Antilla, had a sister ship. Both were designed to use a new means of propulsion. And had been in Galveston before traveling to the Caribbean. The ship was running cargo, mainly sulfur. It was a member of the German Merchant Marine and, as such, was under military control from Germany. At that time, each Captain of each Merchant Marine ship was provided a sealed envelope at the beginning of their voyages from Germany with specific instructions not to open it unless a specific code word was transmitted from Germany. On August 25th, 1939, the word Essberger was broadcast, and the Antilla, along with the other ships, received that message. It instructed all German ships to leave shipping lanes, disguise themselves, fly flags of other countries, and evade any contact if possible. A follow-up message was broadcast on August 28th,1939, instructing all ships to head to German ports or seek refuge in the ports of neutral countries. The Antilla, along with several other ships, attempted to seek refuge in the harbor of Curacao. The harbor was full, and the ships were unable to stay, so they diverted to Aruba, where they moored off Malmok. There were three other ships, the Troja, the Heidelberg, and the Consul Horn, which anchored with the Antilla. All was fine. Aruba was a neutral country until May 10th, 1940, when Germany invaded the Netherlands. War was declared by the Netherlands, and an order to seize German assets was issued. While the ships were anchored, the Governor of Aruba had demanded and confiscated the ships' radio equipment. The ship, he Consul Horn made an escape and ran the British and French blockade and made an escape. The Captain of the Antilla, Captain Schmit, decided not to attempt an escape as the new ship had experienced engine troubles, and he was not confident it could escape. The Antilla was a new ship, and the allies were keen to capture as much tonnage as possible. The Dutch Marines were ordered to seize the ship. The exercise was a mess. The Marines arrived late in the day/early night to capture it. The Captain negotiated for them to return in he morning, as they were supposedly friends, and he would hand over the ship. When the Marines returned, they found the crew had spread oil over the ship and set it on fire to scuttle it. Subsequently, there was a court-martial proceeding in the Netherlands. Over a few years, efforts were explored to raise the ship either as salvage or for scrap iron value. All were abandoned. So, now, folks, it's here in 60 Feet of water for you all to explore."

The passengers gave a round of applause and rushed to receive the snorkeling equipment.

Samantha watched as Sebastiano stripped and donned his snorkel gear. He stood at the rail of the boat with his friend and Sophia. Sophia turned her back to the water and fell backward. Sebastiano followed, then his friend. She continued to watch as Sebastiano reached out and guided Sophia, pointing below to things he observed on the ship. Feeling a little solitary, she decided to join them. Equipped in her snorkeling gear, she plunged into the clear waters.

Sophia saw her first and beckoned her to join them. As a group, they swam and circled over the wreck. The water was clear, and the visibility was perfect. They made out various parts of the ship and observed the huge, ruptured hole where the explosion had taken out a part of the side of the ship. Samantha was fascinated by all the marine life hovering over and at times in the wreck. She pointed out many of the brightly colored fish to Sophia. Time flew by until they heard the warning horn from the boat to return.

Back on the boat, there was excited chatter from the other passengers discussing what they had seen. People stood in small groups drinking, laughing, and smoking. Samantha and Sophia returned to their favorite area near the bow of the boat and sat to dry off. It wasn't long before Sebastiano and his friend, whom he introduced as Carlos Perez, joined them. Sebastiano suggested a white wine, as a luncheon was soon to be served.

The four of them sat, relaxed, and chatted. After the snorkel, Samantha found her anxiety level drop like a stone, and she freely engaged in the conversation.

Sebastiano listened intently as he asked Samantha about Chicago, her job, and her family. Her reluctance to share was gone. Soon, there was laughter, especially as Sophia regaled them with the adventures of her life. The conversation turned around to Sebastiano.

Initially, he was shy and reserved. After prompting from Samantha, he decided to share.

"I am from Paisa in Colombia. My family has owned and operated the plantations for years. We are a major producer. My father is getting older, and one day I will need to take over and run the plantation. It will be a challenge, but I love the work. The business has been good to us."

Samantha found herself becoming more interested in Sebastiano, Colombia, and his family's business. Conversely, he found Samantha just as interesting.

Not to be excluded, Sophia asked about Carlos.

"You may find it strange, but I am here on business. I am a part-owner of a ladies' fashion distributor in Colombia. We represent South American clothing and footwear companies and manage the exports to a number of islands in the Caribbean. Here in Aruba, we have a special retailer. It is called the D Shop. They carry some of our best product lines."

Sophia made a mental note of the name and intended to find the store. The idea of fashion that was different from that which was available in Chicago appealed to her.

Their conversation was interrupted by a crew member calling that lunch was available. A luncheon of chicken and ribs was passed through a porthole below deck, and the passengers sat and stood at different locations to eat and drink.

After lunch, the boat sailed in close to shore at Malmok and close to the famous area, Tres Trapi. The area Tres Trapi, meaning three steps carved in the rock, has a small cave and is known for the turtles that are found there. Both Samantha and Sophia were excited to swim from the boat to see them. They were not disappointed.

Back on the boat, things were livening up. A rope swing had been activated, and passengers of all ages were swinging out from the boat and releasing themselves over the water. A few timid adventurers rode on the backs of a crew member. There were shrieks of laughter and feigned terror.

There was no stopping Sophia, and before long, she was a frequent rope swinger. After some convincing, Samantha joined in.

The boat's horn sounded to advise the remaining swimmers that the sail was over and to return on board for the slow cruise back to shore at Haducarari.

Happy passengers boarded the small boat to be ferried back to the dock. Sebastiano sat next to Samantha.

"I would like to know you more. Would you join me for a drink when we get back to land?"

Samantha laughed.

"You make it sound like we have been on an overseas voyage and are just getting back to land. That's funny."

"I try, but sometimes my English is wrong. I use the wrong words."

Sophia sat quietly and happily watching them talk. She was pleased that, finally, Samantha was interested in mixing with other people. She was shocked when his invitation for drinks was accepted.

"I have my car parked at the dock. I am hoping that you and Sophia will join Carlos and me for a little fun and drinks at the Bugaloe. I will drive us there."

"What is Bugaloe?"

"It is a very popular restaurant and bar on the pier in front of the RIU hotel. Very popular. Sometimes, even in the afternoon, people dance there. It is a happy place and always very busy."

Before Samantha could respond, Sophia accepted.

"Yes, I am in the mood for a little dancing after this cruise. Will we be allowed in since we are in bathing suits?"

"Haha. If you were dressed any other way, I think you would look out of place. It is so casual there."

Back at the dock, Sebastiano and Carlos assisted the ladies up onto the wooden planks of the dock. They walked past the Haducarari restaurant to the car. Monica at the restaurant saw them pass and waved.

"I hope you had a nice sail. Come and dine with us soon," she called.

Samantha was surprised when they reached the car. It was a new pearl cream colored Mercedes. Sebastiano held open the front passenger door for her. Carlos similarly did the same with the rear door for Sophia.

In high spirits, the four left for Bugaloe.

As they drove through the Palm Beach strip, Samantha commented on how deserted it was compared to all the action she had seen the evening before. The strip was deserted.

As they reached the entrance for the walkway down to the beach and restaurant on the pier, they found Alex, from Dushi Tera, and his jeep pulled off on the side of the road. The hood of the jeep was open, and Alex stood with another man, pointing into the engine compartment.

"Sebastiano, please stop. That's Alex. Let's see if we can help."

Samantha left the car and quickly walked back to Alex. She introduced Sebastiano.

"What is wrong?"

"My mechanic friend here thinks there is some dirt blocking the fuel line. Nothing too major, just inconvenient and annoying."

She observed that a strange, unspoken tension seemed to exist between the two men.

Sebastiano spun away and, while walking back to the car, called to Samantha.

"Nothing we can do. He's on his own with that."

"But maybe he needs a ride somewhere. He was so kind and helpful on the tour we did with him. I hate to leave him stranded like that."

"As I said. Nothing we can do."

Alex watched them return to the pearl cream colored Mercedes. Strangely, he found himself wishing for the opportunity to spend more time with Samantha. He dismissed the thought as a silly schoolboy fantasy and turned back to work with the mechanic.

Alex instinctively disliked Sebastiano. He decided to investigate and find a way to create an interference in any relationship developing between Samantha and Sebastiano.

Chapter 14

A Bugaloe afternoon

Most of the lunch crowd had left the restaurant. A few remained at the bar, settled in for a session of drinking and talking with new 'friends'.

The hostess met them and showed them to a covered table at the end of the pier, at the edge of the water. It was a beautiful setting.

While sitting and chatting, tour boats and catamarans docked at the edge of the pier. With each arrival, crowds of passengers disembarked while a queue of others waited to board for the next cruise. The atmosphere was festive.

"Sebastiano, I am interested in how coffee is grown by your family. Can you tell us about it?"

Before he could speak, a waitress arrived to take their drink order.

Loud music started, drowning out any possibility of conversation. They laughed and moved to the rhythm of the music, which was a mix of popular modern and Caribbean steel drum music. The atmosphere was relaxed and partylike.

As their drinks were delivered, a young female employee dressed in a Bugaloe T-shirt walked out onto the area used as a dance floor and started singing to the musical accompaniment of Neil Diamond's 'Sweet Caroline'. She walked from table to table and handed the microphone to a member at each table to sing a verse. There was raucous laughter when some of the renditions were belted out.

The girl reached their table and Sebastiano was selected by her. Initially, he declined, but at her insistence, he took the microphone and burst into song. Both Samantha and Sophia were amazed at his beautiful, melodious voice.

The music stopped playing. Samantha was curious and wanted to know more about growing coffee and Sebastiano's family.

"I was born at the family home. Our plantation started very small as a family farm. My father hired local men to assist in the picking and washing of the cherries."

"Cherries? I thought we were talking about coffee beans."

"Yes, Samantha. When they are harvested, they are called cherries. We use two different methods of harvesting on our plantation. For the cherries that will be used for the premium coffees, we hand-pick. This method is best, but it requires a lot of labor. We also use a vibrating harvester that strips all the cherries from a branch, whether they are ripe or not. We use this method in our larger plantations."

"Why would you pick them if they are not ripe?"

"There is a process of washing, separating, fermenting, and the bad ones are discarded."

"How did your family build such a large business?"

"The government put a lot of pressure on many local farmers to root out their coca plants and grow coffee. The farmers quickly found out they made less than half as much by growing coffee beans rather than the leaves used to make cocaine. A lot were unable to survive, while others were intimidated by armed gangs threatening them if they stopped growing coca and supplying the cartels. The price the collectives paid for coffee was decreasing due to world demand and excess production from other countries, yet the price for coca leaves and cocaine increased. There were killings, and several farmers' homes were set on fire. Those farmers who went back to growing coca faced another problem. The government has reached a deal with the US government to eradicate as much coca growing as they can. Our government sent in armed military thugs who set fire to coca plantations. The government also used planes to spray the fields. That was a problem for us as they often mistook our fields for coca. With all the financial and unsafe conditions the farmers faced, many wanted to sell. My father and my older brothers devised a plan whereby they took over the growing and harvesting, but allowed the farmers to retain a percentage ownership of the land. The farmers loved the arrangement, but others actively threatened us and engaged in creating problems. Our family hired an armed squad to protect the plantations. The farmers still make less money, but their lives have improved. My father insisted on education and set up a medical facility. The conflict between the cartels and our family exists. We are always cautious. Because we are close to Medillin, it is a never-ending threat. We have reached an uneasy agreement with them to leave us alone. Naturally, we needed to make some concessions. I do not wish to discuss those."

"It seems your family lives a risky and turbulent life."

"Samantha, my family roots are hundreds of years old. In our culture, even among the bad guys, there is a certain respect. We leave them alone and at times pretend not to see or know about things, and that way we maintain peace."

The music started again, and Sebastiano reached out to Samantha. Within minutes, they were dancing and laughing. A slow romantic ballad played. Sebastiano placed his hand on her lower back and pulled her to him. She did not resist.

"Sebastiano, I wish to leave here now. I want to go to Eagle Beach and enjoy swimming and sun before it gets too late."

"I will take you there. I will not be able to join you as I have some business matters to attend to. If you like, I will pick you up at Bucuti and Tara. I will have a little surprise for you."

"Will Sophia be with us?"

"If she wishes to join us, then of course."

Samantha was surprised when he embraced her. She had not expected that, but did not pull away. His aura of mystique and handsome looks intrigued her.

"Maybe if we are still friends after I return to Chicago, you can visit me and I will show you my city."

Sebastiano released her and stood back in silence.

"I am afraid that is not possible. Your government has made it impossible. They have placed me on a list of suspected criminals involved in the cocaine trade. My lawyer in Bogota has unsuccessfully attempted to have me removed and their records corrected. We get no cooperation from the US government. We suspect they have me confused with someone with a similar name who is involved with the cartels. We have lobbied, sent information, including my police and military records, but they refuse to correct the problem."

Samantha considered this.

"Is what you are telling me true? I am a lawyer and do have some contacts. I could make a gentle inquiry to personnel I know in those departments. I must be sure, though."

"I cannot ask you to do that. Let's see how our relationship develops. Now, let's ask Sophia if she wants to go to the beach with you."

His response triggered Samantha's natural suspiciousness. Something in his reply did not seem right. Samantha decided extra caution was required on her part. If the relationship developed, she decided to speak with her colleague, Mandy Pine, the firm's liaison and partner who dealt with cases involving the US government and various departments. Mandy's reputation in the legal community was exceptional. If Sebastiano was telling the truth, she would find out. If, on the other hand, he was involved in criminal activities, she would find out.

On the drive from Bugaloe to Eagle Beach, she found herself wondering about him. She questioned his expensive Mercedes car, the gold Rolex watch, and heavy gold chains around his neck, his expensive taste in clothes, the large, flashy horseshoe-shaped gold and diamond ring, and his attitude toward money. Her suspicions continued to grow. What he had told her was disconcerting.

They arrived at Eagle Beach. While Samantha and Sophia were deciding on a location to sit, Sebastiano went to speak with two young men at a shack on the beach. Moments later, they carried two lounge chairs down the beach for the girls and dug in an umbrella for shade.

"Enjoy the rest of your afternoon. Carlos and I must go and look after some matters back home in Colombia. I may try to call you later at the Bucuti."

The men returned to the Mercedes and drove off.

After they settled onto the loungers, Samantha spoke sternly to Sophia.

"Sophia, what Sebastiano told me about Colombia and the family business concerns me. He told me he is unable to travel to the US. His story did not make sense. I suspect those two may not be the nice guys they pretend to be. Please accept what I am saying. I have had years of training to be a lawyer and can decipher what is not being said. He said some things that make me believe he is hiding much more that is sinister. I was shocked when he tried to explain that the family has a private armed squad of men for the protection of the farms. I suspect the protection is for the family. Something is wrong. Do not encourage Carlos any further. Be careful."

Sophia sat wide-eyed, listening.

"I wasn't sure what you were talking about. It seemed intense, and then I watched as he started to make moves on you while dancing. Do you think we are safe?"

"After we swim and sun ourselves a bit, we will walk back to the Bucuti. It's not far, besides you can't take a taxi wet. When we get back, I am going to call Alex and ask if he will join us for a drink and ask him his opinion."

"Good idea. Now let's go and swim."

Back at the Bucuti, Samantha found the card Alex had given her. She punched the numbers into her phone. It was answered by a staticky Alex. The connection was so bad that it dropped. Within a minute, Alex called her back.

"Alex, there is something Sophia and I would like to discuss with you. Are you able to come to the Bucuti?"

"I am just dropping off some guests in Savaneta. I can be there in about thirty minutes."

The girls took showers and waited for Alex to arrive.

They met Alex in the lobby and suggested they go to the resort's bar, the SandBar, which is not open to the public but strictly for guests and their visitors.

After some inconsequential chat, Samantha told him of her concern based on the details Sebastiano had told her. Alex said nothing, but listened intently. When she finished, he paused for a long while before answering.

"Aruba is a beautiful place, and generally, the people are nice. There is, however, an element of our society that operates in shady business. I caution you not to go anywhere alone with these guys. I have some friends who can check them out. Where are they staying?"

"They have suites at the Hyatt. Sebastiano has asked me to join him for a special New Year's Eve dinner at Ruinas del Mar at the Hyatt. Now, I am apprehensive about going."

"Samantha, that is a beautiful restaurant. The restaurant is designed to create the illusion of the old Bushiribana Gold Mill. There is a large lagoon with koi fish, waterfalls, and a stunning rooftop garden filled with flowering bougainvillea. It is a very romantic place. If he invited you there, it will be safe. There will be other diners enjoying the New Year's festivities that the Hyatt is known to have for their guests. I think you should go. Did he indicate what he had planned after the dinner?"

"Yes, he told us we will go up to the lighthouse to see the fireworks at midnight."

"Let me check on a few things. Now, do you and Sophia have any dinner plans? I have an idea you might enjoy."

"No. We thought of going to the Palm Beach strip, but I would prefer something not so crowded. Since it is New Year's, I suspect it will be very busy."

"That is good, then, because what I am considering is quiet. It is something Aruba is known for, and I doubt you will forget it."

"What is it?"

"Something special. Now you don't need to get all dressed up. Shorts and flip-flops are fine. Just what you are wearing. We should leave soon. I will need to make a stop on the way."

In Alex's jeep, they headed toward Palm Beach but turned inland. At a small roadside shack, Alex stopped and jumped from the jeep. It was several minutes later that he returned to the jeep with paper bags of delicious-smelling food. Again, he stopped at a small convenience store and bought two bottles of cold white wine.

Samantha was curious.

"Where are we going?"

"Very soon you will know."

They drove on and up the coast. At Malmok, Alex wheeled the jeep over to an area shaded by trees and stopped.

"Now, ladies, we will have a dinner of real Aruban food with wine while we watch Aruba's magnificent sunset."

Alex pulled portable beach chairs from the back of the jeep and set them up under a palapa on the beach.

Samantha sat, kicking up the pure white sand with her bare feet and laughing at the jokes and light-hearted conversation. Alex fussed around the girls, offering different foods for which he provided detailed descriptions.

"There are not a lot of original Aruban foods. We have pastechi and Keshi yena, and used to make iguana soup before the government made that illegal. Most foods here are influenced by people who have moved here from Colombia or Venezuela. You will find empanadas, arepas, and other foods.

The sun had started to dip toward the horizon. In the sky overhead, layers of cloud were reflected in orange and pink layers.

Sophia raised her glass and proposed a toast as the sun changed to a huge glowing orange ball and slipped below the horizon.

They remained on the beach as twilight filled the sky with a soft, glowing light. It was dark when Alex dropped them back at the Bucuti.

Chapter 15

New Year's Eve, December 31st

The Day Trip

Samantha met Sophia for breakfast at the Elements restaurant. Neither were hungry after the feast of local food they had enjoyed with Alex. They ordered fresh espresso coffees and fresh fruit platters. Both were relaxed and in great moods.

"Sophia, there are so many things to see that we could easily do by ourselves. I asked at the concierge desk, and even though it's the high season, it is possible to get a rental car for the day, as there was a cancellation. Let's go adventuring alone for the day."

Armed with a tourist map and guide provided with the rental car, they set out for the day.

Their first stop was at the California Lighthouse. Samantha declined, but Sophia, full of energy, elected to purchase a ticket to climb the 123 stairs to the top of the lighthouse.

Alone, Samantha walked around and explored the area. To the east, she saw the surf crashing against the rocks along the barren east coast. Looking to the north, she was amazed by the bright white sands of the dunes, and when she looked south, she saw the curved line of beaches. She attempted to remember the beach's different names. There was Arashi, Boca Catalina, Palm Beach, and off in the distance, she made out the different resorts lining Eagle Beach.

With the strong, constant wind blowing, the temperature of the hot sun beating down did not trouble her. She was feeling fully relaxed and appreciating life.

Her moment of serenity was shattered by the return of Sophia.

"Well, that was amazing. I think that climbing up those stairs has solved last night's Margarita effects. I'm ready to hit the road again. I'm feeling very religious. Let's find the chapel that is in the tour guide and map."

"You? Feeling religious? Oh boy! I am wondering what this Aruba trip is doing to us?"

"I gotta find me an Aruban hunk and move here. To hell with Chicago and all the winds and cold and snow. Nope, I'm convinced. Now I just need a real man here."

"Sophia, you are incorrigible."

They drove slowly down from the lighthouse, swerving to miss some huge potholes, and continued through an area called Malmok, following the directions on the map. After passing through the Palm Beach strip, they turned inland and followed the cactus-lined road up to the Halto Vista Chapel. On the way, Sophia freaked at the sight of a large dead Boa snake on the highway.

"You better keep any fucker like that miles away from me or I won't need a plane to get back home."

Samantha laughed. Behind Sophia's bravado was a vulnerable soul. She truly appreciated her friend, who was direct and truthful.

Soon, the road twisted, and they arrived at white crucifixes lining the roadside. The road crested, and off in the distance, they saw the dark blue waters of the Atlantic stretching out to the horizon.

The road abruptly ended and twisted to a parking area in front of the small and unique chapel.

A group of tourists stood around a souvenir seller and a local with a cart selling coconut drinks. There was a large contingent of ATVs parked, and some people walking to visit inside the chapel. Samantha was disgusted.

"Sophia, the guide says that this is an active church and place of worship for the locals. I am appalled to see shirtless men carrying cans of beer entering the church, and scantily dressed women. This is not right. It disturbs me. Let's leave."

Samantha studied the map and decided to continue the adventure with a trip to Savaneta and later to Baby and Rogers Beach.

They backtracked from the Chapel through an area called Noord and proceeded down through the main area of Oranjestad. There were 3 cruise ships in port. Passengers from the ships lined the sidewalks and crossed the street, slowing the traffic to explore the various stores. Samantha decided to park, walk around, explore, and admire the old Dutch Colonial architecture.

After an hour, they continued their drive towards the south end of the island. Their drive took them past the airport and later the water and electricity plant.

"Samantha, at the next roundabout, turn right. This tour guide suggests driving along the shore until we reach an area named Mangel Halto. There is a beach and a local bar. Let's stop there for a bit. It could be fun to mix with the locals."

"Honestly, Sophia, I think you will have visited every bar on the island before we go home."

"Damn you, Samantha. Why did you mention home? I don't want to think about it."

The road dipped and turned. A narrow bridge took them over Spans Lagoon. They drove on, and to their right, the bright blue waters of the Caribbean sparkled. Within minutes, they arrived at an area dotted with palapas and people swimming. Samantha turned into a parking area of a local bar with the name Mangel Halto spelled incorrectly. She smiled, "Now I'm seeing some real Aruba," she thought.

By the time Samantha returned from a short walk to look at the scenery, Sophia was already at the bar and talking to one of the several locals either sitting or standing near her, drinking beers.

The local was involved in a serious conversation with Sophia, explaining the differences between the local beers.

"This is Balashi. Nice beer. It's a pilsener. Now this other one is a favorite called Chill. Much lighter than Balashi and a great drink for these hot days. Now this one might interest you. It's called Magic Mango, and as the name suggests, it's a fruity, tasty beer. It was created by our brewery's first lady brewmaster. Popular brew for the visiting young ladies. We also make rum, vodka, wine, and other drinks on the island, but I'm just a beer guy."

Samantha had listened to the description and decided to try a Magic Mango, while Sophia selected a Chill.

A friendly spectacled Chinese lady behind the bar reached into a gigantic chiller below the bar and produced their drinks. The bottles were placed on the bar in front of them.

"Don't ask. Look around. Everyone is drinking from the bottle. Forget asking for a glass, Samantha. Just go with the locals."

Samantha laughed and put the bottle to her lips. As she did so, a series of loud explosions sounded from outside the bar. All the locals, beers in hand, rushed out the doors. There was laughter and loud bantering between the men. Both Samantha and Sophia were confused. Out on the road, several men stood back from a snake-like object spitting flame and explosions. Smoke filled the air, and the snake burned along the surface of the road. While they watched, another series of continuous explosions occurred at a building a little further away. Sophia asked the local who had explained the beers what it all meant.

"Dear, that's the lighting of the pagara. A pagara is a long string of firecrackers that we Arubans light at the end of the year. The lighting of the pagara scares away any evil spirits from entering a home or business. It is a New Year's custom here on the island. Where are you ladies going after here?"

"We are driving down to Rogers Beach and through San Nicolaas."

"Expect to see lots of pagaras then. Most shops and businesses will have them. You will see lots in San Nicolaas."

Eager to see San Nicolaas, they continued their drive. Sophia buried her head in the tour guide. They approached an area with cars parked on both sides of the road and in a large parking area. She noticed a black flag with a skull and crossbones flying at the entrance to a building. She consulted her guide.

"Samantha, that is a place called Zeerovers. Fresh fish restaurant on the water. Sounds good. Should we stop and visit?"

Samantha slowed and looked in the entrance. A log queue of tourists stood waiting to place their orders. She decided against it.

"Sophia. It is really busy, and we want to see more of this end of the island before we head back. Remember, we have that special New Year's dinner with Sebastiano and Carlos at the Hyatt tonight. We must watch our time. Maybe we can make a trip back to Zeerovers another day when we don't have a schedule."

As they continued their drive, they passed the Dutch Marine Barracks in Savaneta and, within minutes, arrived in San Nicolaas. They were amazed at all the chimney stacks, storage tanks, and other processing equipment at the old oil refinery. Sophia read out information about the refinery and how it had been important during the war.

A sign pointed them into downtown San Nicolaas. They slowly drove down a narrow street, amazed at the bright, large murals painted on many of the buildings, including the Police Station. Samantha pulled he car over and parked.

"Let's walk for a while and see these murals. They are amazing."

After spending close to an hour exploring San Nicolaas, they left to continue to Baby and Rogers Beaches.

They followed the signs and were soon driving the road leading to the beaches. There were no houses or buildings. It was an open space with a view of the surf from the Atlantic crashing against the shore and huge towers of spray shooting up high. Their drive was interrupted when they turned a corner and encountered half a dozen donkeys on the road. They stopped. Sophia opened her window, and soon a donkey's head pushed into the car, looking for a carrot or apple.

"Samantha, we need to come back here and bring them some food. Let's plan it, and we can stop at Zeerovers."

"Yes, we will do that, but there is so much more for us to see. I am not sure we will be able to visit other places before we leave. We will run out of time. I never expected to find so many interesting places on such a small island. Maybe I will need to come back."

Sophia nodded and agreed.

The donkeys sauntered off to another car that had stopped in their search for food, and the girls continued on their drive.

It was only a few-minute drive before they encountered a small incline leading down to the beaches. Signs pointed to Rogers and Baby Beach. Samantha selected Rogers Beach. The road led into a deserted, long, curved white sand beach. Small local fishing boats were moored at one end of the beach. A small pier ran from the shore out into the ocean, and local boys were jumping from it into the water. Samantha parked, and she and Sophia waded in the warm, crystal-clear water. Sophia turned to her and exclaimed:

"I would like to swim, but I don't have my bikini. Maybe I can go naked. No one is around."

"Sophia, I read that nudity is not allowed at beaches here on the island."

"What are they going to do?"

Sophia whipped off her clothing and plunged into the water. While she was swimming, a police patrol car passed by. Samantha cringed, but it kept going along to the end of the beach before turning and driving away.

"Sophia. Get out. That was too close."

Laughing, Sopia emerged from the water and ran back to the car. She stood in the sun, shielded by the open door of the car, and dried off.

They drove back and took the road into Baby Beach. Unlike Rogers Beach, the parking lot was full, and hundreds of people were swimming. Samantha looked at the beach and decided not to stop as there were too many people. She continued along the dusty dirt road and came to an open area dotted with hundreds of crosses marking graves. Sophie scrambled through the guide and found the information.

"It is called Pet Cemetery. It is where the locals come to bury their pets."

On the makeshift crosses, the names of pets were painted or scrawled on in marker pen.

"How unique and endearing. Such respect. I am impressed."

They continued, and the road started to gradually climb. They soon reached an elevated plateau that looked north along the east coast. Even at a distance, they viewed the wild waves crashing against the rocky shore, sending huge plumes of spray into the air where the wind then carried it inland.

Done with exploring, they decided to head back to the resort. On the road back from the beaches, they arrived at a huge red anchor and followed the dirt road past it and down to a surf beach named Boca Grande. Several windsurfers plied the waters. Along the shore, they observed huts built on the rugged beach. The huts were very basic and built from scrounged materials. Further off in the distance, they saw a large wind power farm and decided to investigate. They drove the rough, pitted dirt road. Along the way, they encountered two herds of goats. The goats stopped and apprehensively looked at their car. The road stopped and turned up a hill, and soon they found themselves returning to a highway leading back to San Nicolaas.

The afternoon was still early, and while driving back to the resort, a sign caught their attention. A hand-painted sign pointed down a small side road to a local restaurant named Batata.

"Samantha, I am a little hungry and thirsty. Let's stop for a beer and a snack."

They drove down the road, following the signs, and found a small restaurant on the sand of the beach. Chairs and tables were arranged beneath sheltered palapas. A friendly waitress greeted them. Sophia laughed when she read the waitress's name…Sophia. Naturally, this led to an immediate conversation.

The restaurant was not busy, with half a dozen other locals seated and drinking beers. They selected a table at the edge of the seating that looked out to the water, and ordered two bottles of Chill beer, and orders of quesadillas and chicken wings.

"We need to eat lightly, as we have that special dinner at the Hyatt this evening."

For the next hour, they sat talking about the trip and how it was nothing like what they had assumed.

With the afternoon sun starting to set, they finished up at Batata and drove their way back to Bucuti and Tara resort in traffic that was heavier than they had experienced driving down to the beaches.

"Sophia, I am going to go and take a shower and rest. It is going to be a long night tonight."

Chapter 16

New Year's Eve night

Fireworks (and Fireworks)

Sebastiano and Carlos arrived at Bucuti and Tara resort to take Samantha and Sophia to the New Year's dinner at the Hyatt. The chef had arranged a special menu for the evening.

Samantha was seated in the front with Sebastiano, while Sophia sat with Carlos in the back. The interior of the Mercedes was spacious and elegant.

They had dressed as festively as possible, given the limited clothing they had brought on the trip.

Upon pulling up at the entrance to the hotel, a valet quickly approached to assist them from the car and to take and park the Mercedes.

They walked up the steps and into the expansive lobby area of the hotel. Several staff members who knew Sebastiano as a guest of some importance greeted him. A manager walked briskly toward them and addressed Sebastiano.

"I understand you will be joining us for the special New Year's dinner this evening. I have personally arranged a special table for you and your guests. Let me take you to the restaurant."

He guided the group down a steep set of stairs to a reception desk at the entrance of the restaurant. A hostess stood at the desk. The manager spoke with her and then escorted them into the restaurant and out through the doors leading to a large patio area.

The restaurant, named Ruinas del Mar, was exclusive. It was fashioned to reflect the ruins of the old gold mine. High stone walls, treated to look aged and weathered, rose around two sides. On top of the walls, prolific bougainvillea grew, forming a roof garden with their bright and magnificent blooms, creating a tropical atmosphere. A waterfall tumbled down the stone facing, and water crashed into a huge pond. In the pond, large colored koi fish swam lazily around. Several black swans gracefully drifted on the surface of the pond.

The manager had reserved a table beside the pond, where the soft sound of water dropping from the waterfall into the pond provided a serene effect.

Samantha sat absorbing the surroundings, amazed at how tranquil the restaurant was, especially on this festive night.

A waiter arrived at the table to take drink orders. Sebastiano asked the others for their preferences and then selected a bottle of Dom Pérignon.

After the champagne was delivered, they sat making small talk until the maitre d arrived at the table.

"Welcome. Tonight we have a very special menu prepared by Chef Charles. The dinner consists of 5 courses.

The first course features Seared jumbo scallops.
They are served with Citric Sour Cream and Caviar, Rustic Artichoke Pesto with Pinolis and Fresh Basil.

The second course is a creamy lobster Pomodoro bisque, Lobster Meat, and Pesto.

For the third course, he has prepared Caribbean tuna tiradito with Passion Fruit Leche de Tigre, Red Onion, Mixed Bell Peppers, Lemon, and Microgreens.

For the fourth, the main course, you may select either Beef tenderloin & lobster with Cauliflower Mousseline, Grilled Oyster Mushrooms, Garlic Butter, and Mixed Peppercorn Sauce,

Or Grilled salmon & tiger shrimp, served with Creamy Polenta, Crispy Bacon, Rainbow Mini Beets, and a Classic Gremolata.

Finally, the fifth and final course is a delightful Black Forest mousse cake. Chef Charles' version of Black Forest Cake with Pastry Cream, Assorted Fresh Berries, and Chocolate Ice Cream.

We pride ourselves on this evening's special menu. Let me know when you wish to order."

Soft music played quietly in the background, enhancing the gentle sound of the falling water. Samantha considered it the perfect setting for the special dinner. She was, however, still wary of Sebastiano. There was something he had said that had caused her to be cautious.

She was aware of Sophia watching her discreetly, but not saying anything. Instead, she engaged Carlos in a meaningless conversation about his business in ladies' clothing. Samantha saw that Carlos was bored with the conversation.

Samantha also watched a small group of men at the entrance to the patio. They did not seem to fit the occasion or the place. They were all dressed in normal attire. Nothing special for the evening. She had noticed them watching their group several times. At one point, one of the men stepped onto the patio with a professional camera and took photos. He aimed at the swans and the exterior décor of

Ruinas del Mar, but Samantha swore she saw him point the camera in their direction on more than one occasion. One of the men appeared to be watching Sophia. He was young, maybe 40 years of age, and good-looking with his cropped blonde hair. Samabtha decided he was Dutch and probably on Christmas vacation away from the cold winter weather of the Netherlands.

They ordered their meals. The ladies ordered the Grilled Salmon and shrimp, and the men selected the Beef Tenderloin.

The conversation died off while they enjoyed the food. After dinner, Sebastiano ordered drinks.

"We will need to leave soon. There will be a crowd up at the lighthouse to see the fireworks. It's a great location. The whole island is visible. At midnight, it is as if the island catches fire. There are rockets, special exploding shells, and many other displays. Something you ladies will never forget."

It was almost 11:00 pm when Sebastiano charged the dinner to his room and suggested they leave. By the time they reached the front entrance, the Mercedes had been delivered back and was waiting for them. The valet had left the air conditioning running to cool the car for them. Samantha appreciated the cool interior of the car.

After a short ten-minute drive, they climbed the hill up to the lighthouse. A huge crowd had gathered to view the fireworks. Sebastiano inched his way through the crowd and parked the Mercedes behind the lighthouse on a flat area of land.

They left the car and walked toward the side facing Palm Beach. As they made their way through the crowd, men offered Samantha and Sophia all types of drinks............beer, whiskey, wine, champagne, and more. The mood was friendly, and on a couple of occasions, Sophia did accept and chugged from an offered bottle. It was a party. The locals were in a happy and festive mood. Some in the crowd let off fireworks, and some planted wine bottles in the soil and fired small rockets, to the delight of the young children running around.

As midnight approached, the crowd quietened a little. At the stroke of midnight, the island lit up. All down the coast, rockets soared into the air. In front of the Hotels, the specially constructed displays burst into masses of color and pyrotechnics. Inland, more rockets soared up from private homes.

Samantha moved close to Sophia and hugged her.

"Happy New Year, my friend. I am so happy you came. This is magnificent."

She had no sooner spoken those words when all hell broke loose. Blue lights on three dark cars commenced flashing, and a high-intensity light mounted on a van shone on them. Through the blinding light, Samantha was able to make out the figures of several men running at them with guns drawn. She shrank. A rough pair of hands grabbed her and pushed her to the ground. She heard Sophia scream. To her right, she made out several large cops tackling Sebastiano while twisting his arm and handcuffing him. Carlos took off running with some cops chasing behind him.

A tall cop stood in front of her and extended his hand to lift her, while another handcuffed her, then Sophia.

"We are the Narcotics Unit of the Aruba Police and the Police Arrest Team. We are arresting you on suspicion of drug trafficking. You are being detained and will be taken to the police station in Shaba for questioning. There will be a prosecutor at the station."

"You are making a mistake. My friend and I are tourists. We are visiting from the States."

"You can tell your story at the station. I need your ID and passports. Now, please get into the rear of the van."

Loud sobs rose from Sophia.

"Sophia. It is all a mistake. I am sure it will be solved quickly. Please try to be calm."

They were assisted into the van for the trip to the police station. Sebastiano was taken away separately. The van rocked unevenly as it drove down from the lighthouse area. They were thrown around as it pitched and rolled side to side. Once the van reached the paved road, the ride became smoother. Samantha looked at Sophia. She was concerned that Sophia was going into shock. She banged on the wall separating them from the driver and shouted that she needed help. The van slowed and stopped. The cops opened the door and saw Sophia's condition and immediately called for an ambulance. They sat Sophia up and tried to calm her.

An ambulance arrived, and the paramedics assessed the situation and injected a sedative to calm her. They hooked up monitors and took blood pressure, heart rate, and other readings. A stocky young cop stood beside her and took her hand. He removed his police cap, and Samantha recognized him as one of the men who had been watching them at the Hyatt. He was the blonde one she thought was Dutch. He looked at Samantha and introduced himself.

"I am Officer Jan van der Brekel. I will make sure your friend is treated well."

"Why have we been arrested? We have done nothing."

" You were with two of Colombia's top drug lords. We have been trying to arrest them for a long while. We have no record of them entering the island. How do you know them?"

Samantha told the officer about the evening at Sopranos and the Jolly Pirares trip. He asked their names and laughed when Samantha identified Sebastiano.

"No, his name is Pedro dela Cruz. He is a major player in the drug cartels. He is a ruthless murderer. Who did they say the other one was?"

"They introduced him as Carlos Perez. Who is he?"

"His name is Hermano Santiago. He is an enforcer for several cartels. He is the executioner of the peasant farmers who do not produce or are suspected of informing the authorities. He is sadistic and extremely cruel. His executions are grotesque and performed that way to intimidate others who might be thinking of trying to leave the trade. It is sick that he has a very religious name."

"We had no idea. I am a lawyer, and when Sebastiano was describing his life in Colombia, he said things that concerned me. With my legal training, I can often determine what the truth is, but I wasn't completely sure. We should not have accepted that dinner invitation for tonight."

Jan looked down at her leg and noticed the blood running down her leg.

"Let me get a paramedic. You are bleeding. Sit on the back ledge of the van."

The paramedic rolled up her dress and immediately sterilized a deep gash on her knee that had been caused when she was forced to the ground. He applied some gauze and a bandage."

"This is not good. We will have to report this and fill in many pages of details. When someone is injured during an arrest, it is always a major incident."

"What will happen now?"

"We will continue to the station. It will be hectic. New Year's and there will be a lot of drunks and noise. Be prepared. You will be questioned, and if you can establish what you have told me, then I am sure you will be released without delay."

"What about my friend?"

"We will ask the ambulance to take her. They will observe her. I will speak with the chief. It may be possible for you to return to your resort. They will probably want your passports until it is understood that you are innocent and not involved with that gang. Do you want to have your knee checked at the hospital emergency department?"

"I should be fine. Ask the paramedics for some antiseptic cream and some bandages. I will look after it."

She watched as Jan left her to spend time with Sophia. He expressed genuine concern for her. He returned to Samantha.

"Has she had anxiety attacks or any other problems that we should be aware of? The paramedics are concerned. She can be admitted for observation. They need to know her medical history if you can help. Does she take any medications? Does she do drugs? Her blood pressure is high with signs of hypertension."

"No, I can confirm she does not do drugs, and I am unaware of her taking any medication."

"As commanding officer of this operation, I am ordering the ambulance to take her to the hospital for observation. She will be accompanied by two officers until she is cleared of any wrongdoing. I can arrange for you to be with her, but you will still be under arrest. You will both be under guard."

The other cops were standing together, talking and laughing. Jan van der Brekel seemed to be the only one concerned about their well-being. She noticed his concern for Sophia and was curious.

He walked over and spoke with some of the other officers, and finally pointed at two of them and pointed to the ambulance. They walked over and started a conversation with the paramedics.

Samantha watched as Sophia was placed on a gurney and loaded into the rear of the ambulance. Jan van der Brekel walked over to her.

"I have arranged for you to join her at the hospital. Two officers will accompany you. I will be in contact before you leave the hospital. Do not try anything foolish. You can ride in the back of the ambulance with Sophia and the officers."

The ride to the hospital was short. During the trip, the officers engaged Samantha in conversation and asked about her association with Sebastiano. They listened intently and exchanged looks. At the hospital, Sophia was taken from the ambulance and placed in a wheelchair. For security, she was handcuffed to the chair. As Samanntha was about to complain, she too was handcuffed and led into the hospital like a common criminal. She resolved that someone would answer for the indignities she and Sophia had experienced that night. Sophia was wheeled to a darkened room and lifted to a bed. The handcuffs were then attached to the side rails of the bed. Samantha felt anger growing in her.

A young doctor entered the room and looked at the chart the paramedics had left. He took her blood pressure and performed a series of procedures. He called for a nurse and instructed that a drip be installed for Sophia. Without a word, he turned and left.

Samantha sat handcuffed in an uncomfortable chair. Outside in the corridor, the two cops sat laughing and drinking coffee. Samantha's anger grew. She noticed that Sophia's breathing had slowed and she had fallen into a sleep. The monitor displaying her blood pressure and heart rate had fallen. She thanked God for the improvement. Now, she decided, it was time to end this.

She heard the cops outside stop talking and heard another person join them. There were murmured voices. The door opened, and Jan van der Brekel entered.

" How is she? I have good news for you. Our checks of your passports, both here with Immigration and with Interpol, show you are clean and therefore free to go. We verified your legitimate entry into Aruba. During the initial interrogation of 'Sebastiano', he admitted they had picked up you and Sophia at the piano bar and gone on the Jolly Pirates cruise with you. He stated he had never met you before. I just need to sign a release and arrange to transport you both back to your resort. You will receive a formal apology from the Department. We try hard, but sometimes mistakes get made. Sorry. Our people were eager to arrest those two, and the adrenaline was pumping. We have been chasing them for years. They have accomplices here who have been able to shield them from us. We did receive a tip advising us of your plans to have dinner with them. That is what led to us ambushing them tonight."

"Who tipped you? No one knew we were going to dinner with them."

"Well, yes, there was a person. We will keep that information secret for that person's protection."

Samantha thought about it and slowly realized who it was.

Back at Bucuti, she sat out on the balcony with a very reserved Sophia. There were still a few fireworks lighting the sky.

"Sophia, we certainly had some fireworks tonight."

"An experience we can talk about for years. Drug lords and cartels. Arrested. An ambulance ride. Time in an Aruban hospital. No one will believe us."

"OK. Happy New Year. I'm off to bed. We have another full day tomorrow."

Chapter 17

New Year's Day

Early morning breakfast on the beach. Sophia was back and in fine form.

"It's New Year's Day, so let's start the year with a bang. Mimosas and Eggs Benedict, but first a plate of fresh fruit. A girl's got to be careful and look after her figure. Still trying to catch that ideal man."

Samantha laughed. Partly out of relief that Sophia was fine, and secondly, because what could have turned into a nasty situation with the police did not.

She was surprised to see Jan van der Brekel striding down the sand toward them.

"Now what? I thought we were through with him."

"Good morning, ladies. I decided to stop in and see how you both are after last night's fiasco. Samantha, how is your knee? Show me, please. It looks bruised."

"Hey, what's wrong with my knees? Want to take a look at them while you are at it? I'm the one you should be concerned about. Want to check my wrists from those handcuffs or other parts where I was mishandled?

Samantha stared at her.

"Sophia, Jan came to visit. I guess the police are worried about what we might do or say."

"No. I am not on police duty. I came because I was concerned, especially about lovely Sophia. It's my day off."

Sophia examined him. Out of uniform, he was attractive with his short-cropped blonde hair, steel grey eyes, and muscular frame. She considered that he may be a catch.

"Thank you for coming. We are fine. Would you care for a New Year's drink?"

Sophia purred the words out, but decided to be careful after the experience with Sebastiona and Carlos.

"Tell me about you, Jan. Are you married to some pretty Dutch girl?

Jan's face darkened, and he averted her eyes.

"No, my fiancée was killed in an accident in the Netherlands. We had planned to marry. I did not want to stay there and live with the memory, and that is why I have moved to Aruba. How about you ladies?"

"No. Not so lucky in the romance department. It seems betrayals followed us both, and in major ways."

"How so? What happened?"

"I thought I was safe. Married a vicar and all. Imagine my surprise when I went home early one day and found him fucking two of his dedicated parishioners in our bed."

"Sophia!. Don't be so brash."

Jan laughed.

"Don't worry. Sometimes it's best to be direct. So then, is there no love interest at present, Sophia?"

"No, I am flying solo."

"A pretty girl like you won't be alone for long. What about you, Samantha?"

"Complicated. He was the desire of all the women in our office. He had everything. Looks, money, and a great legal career, then he got greedy and committed fraudulent actions involving the firm's trust accounts and also my trust accounts. He forged documents and has committed serious fraud."

"Wow. You ladies haven't been lucky. What are your plans for today?"

"After yesterday, we were thinking of a quiet day. Some beach time. Visit a bar or two. Not much."

"If I might be so bold, can I take you to see a couple of things unique to Aruba at this time of year?"

"Will it be safe? We won't get arrested again?"

"Not a chance. Where we will go is very casual. You will be safe."

Jan checked his watch.

"It's too soon, so let's have more drinks, and then we will leave."

" I need to go back to my room for a bit. I will meet you and Sophia in the lobby."

Samantha returned to her room and, in the privacy of the room, called her mother in Illinois. All was well with her mother. She wished her a Happy New Year and hung up and left to join Sophia and Jan.

She found them checking items in the gift shop. They left and walked a short distance to Jan's BMW SUV.

"In Aruba, the locals celebrate New Year's differently from other places in the world. I hope to be able to show you some of those. You will enjoy seeing and participating."

They pulled away from the resort and drove along a crowded Eagle Beach. Samantha identified many local families there, swimming and enjoying the day. As they reached the Palm Beach intersection, Sophia commented on the red color of the road.

"Yes, Sophia. That red is what is left from all the spent firecrackers. In a day or two, it will be gone, either blown or washed away by rain."

Jan turned and drove to the parking area for customers of the Old Mill restaurant. Outside the restaurant was a collection of motorcycles. Samantha was concerned.

"Are we going in there? Is that a motorbike gang? Will we be safe in there?"

"Yes. The motorbike gangs here are mainly groups of friends with motorbikes as their common interest. You will find doctors, accountants, politicians, and other professionals as members. There are even some lawyers. Now wait, as it will get more interesting."

While walking to the entrance of the restaurant, there was a thundering roar in the distance that was growing louder. Jan smiled and pointed out to the road. Approximately a hundred or more motorbikes turned and drove in a long line into the restaurant parking area. The riders dismounted from their bikes. High fives were given along with some members hugging others. The riders started into the pub. It was noisy. Shouts of greetings and laughter filled the air. Samantha watched as some of the riders carried in instruments.

"Jan, what are they doing?"

"In a moment, you will see. They are preparing for Dande. It is a custom here amongst locals. A group of friends or neighbors gets together and plays and sings. You will notice that some are playing instruments that are unique to Aruba. The musicians will pass a hat to collect money. Those who give money do it for good luck. The music is traditional Aruban, and there will be a couple of waltzes. It is customary that the host of the place where the Dande takes place will give the musicians drinks. The music group will go from home to home, or location to location, and play.

While the musicians were assembling in a corner of the restaurant to play, two men carried a box outside and spread a log pagara across in front of the restaurant and neighboring properties. They lit the pagara, and the firecrackers exploded, shooting flames, bits of spent firework containers into the air. The smoke smelled of sulfur and gunpowder. When the pagara finished burning, the musicians started playing. In minutes, some of the men took their women partners and danced to the lively native music.

Sophia clapped her hands and pulled Jan onto the floor to dance. Samantha was thrilled to experience the Dande. When the group stopped playing, they filed out and returned to their bikes before roaring off to the next location.

Jan returned to where Samantha had stood watching the performance. He had his arm firmly around a smiling Sophia's waist. Samantha quickly realized a friendship was developing. She was happy for Sophia.

"If we drive up to the main Noord road later, you will see the Aruba motorbike ride. There will be hundreds of motorbikes in the parade, which is a drive around Aruba. Some money is collected along the route and donated to charity."

Both Samantha and Sophia thanked Jan for taking them to experience a true Aruba experience.

"Let us drive up to Moomba Beach. That is where you were for the Jolly Pirate cruise. We should hurry. It is the New Year's Day Polar Bear plunge. There will be many people participating. Maybe a thousand. They are given an orange toque to wear, and as a group, they all run down the beach and into the water. When they come out of the water, the swimmers are provided with a small cup of Dutch soup to 'warm up'."

"That sounds fun. Can we join in as well and take the plunge?"

"Yes, of course. You will dry off quickly, and I always carry towels in my car that you can use."

Samantha was happy. After last night's drama, this is exactly the type of day she had hoped for.

They arrived at Moomba's and found all parking areas full. Jan left them in his car and went into a building. He returned and drove to a lowered access arm restricting traffic. As he approached, the arm raised, and he drove in, turned, and parked. He did not comment. They jumped out of the SUV and headed to join the excited crowd on the beach. A young boy was distributing the orange toques.

Two men stood with a make-shift rope holding the participants back until noon. A whistle blew, signifying noon, and the crowd ran en masse into the shallow, warm waters. Shrieks of laughter filled the air. Groups splashed water at each other. Within minutes,

Samantha and Sophia were soaked. Sophia found particular joy in splashing a shirtless Jan. Her happiness was clear.

After a while, they climbed from the water and joined the queue for the free Dutch soup. Jan fetched towels from his car, and they sat at the beach drying off.

Sophia loudly announced she was hungry, and Jan smiled before he responded.

"I have a nice place we can visit. It is very close to Bucuti. It is the Costa Linda Beach Resort. Years ago, when I first came to the island, I bought a unit there. I own several weeks. It is my place to escape police work and relatives. Let me take you there. We can have lunch at the Water's Edge restaurant, then spend time on the beach. The beach there is magnificent."

They all agreed and piled back into the car for the short trip to the Costa Linda.

Jan parked, and the three of them walked toward the entrance. Before they made it inside, a friendly man ran out and embraced Jan.

"Jan, welcome. It is so good to see you. It has been a whole month. Who are your friends?"

"Let me introduce Samantha and Sophia. I am showing them around today. We have come for lunch and time on the beach. I guess it is busy since it is New Year's. Ladies, this is Wilmer. He has been here at the Costa Linda for many years and almost knows every owner by name, where they live in the States or Canada, and the names of their family members. He is a loved fixture here."

"It is my pleasure, ladies. Is this your first visit to Aruba? How are you liking it?"

Before they could answer, Jan spoke.

"I am going to the management office. Since we wish to use the beach, I will need to ask for a pass. If it is too busy, we may not be able to enjoy the palapas on the beach. Wilmer, can you look after these two while I'm gone?"

Wilmer regaled them with stories of Aruba and his adventures.

Ten minutes passed before a smiling Jan returned.

"Luck is with us today, we have a pass. It is not always possible to get one during the busy season."

Wilmer went behind his desk. He picked up a two-way radio and made contact with someone. They were unable to understand the conversation as he spoke rapidly in the local Papiamento language. He was smiling when he ended the call.

"Jan, I just spoke with Yipsy, the beach attendant at the towel hut. She told me there is a group who are getting ready to leave, so you will be able to use their palapa."

"But Wilmer. We are having lunch first, and I am sure some others will want the palapa."

"Don't worry. Charlotte, the beach waitress, will take your food and drink orders, and the food will be delivered to the palapa. Just go and see Yipsy at the hut. She is waiting."

They thanked Wilmer and went to meet Yipsy. She took some fresh towels and escorted them to the palapa. It was in a prime location up from the edge of the water with an unobstructed view of the ocean. They arranged the sun loungers and collapsed onto them. For the girls, it was a perfect day.

They didn't wait long before Charlotte, the young, friendly waitress, arrived and handed them a menu, and waited to take their food and drink orders.

Samantha and Sophia ordered Shrimp Louie Salads, and Jan ordered a double order of chicken wings. For drinks, they all ordered Margaritas.

After lunch, they rested awhile and spent the afternoon swimming in the ocean or sunning. At one point, when Jan and Sophia were engaged in a suggestive conversation, Samantha quietly left them on the beach and went to explore the Costa Linda. She spent a little time checking out the tropical plants in the well-groomed gardens, and then checked inside, where she found terminals set up for guests and owners to access the Internet or other sites. There was a coffee shop with tempting cakes and desserts. On a whim, she decided to take an elevator up to the top floor and stand on the common area balcony overlooking the pool and grounds. The overall cleanliness of the resort impressed her. On her way back to the beach, she passed the small sales office. Out of curiosity, she stopped to look at the units listed for sale.

While looking at the list of rental units, an elderly man walked up beside her. He scanned the list and shook his head.

"Damn. I was hoping there would be some units listed for sale. I need to get some price comparisons."

Samantha studied the old man before speaking. His face was kind and portrayed a certain intelligence and life experience.

"Are you looking to buy here? I assume you are retired and would enjoy the beach and Aruba's weather."

"Sadly not, Dearie. My dear wife Ruth and I enjoyed it here for many years. She died three months ago, and I am getting too old, so it is time to sell."

"I might be interested in buying. Do you have time for a coffee? We can sit outside the little coffee shop on the patio and talk."

"My dear, I have all the time in the world and nothing to do. Yes, let's talk."

She extended her hand, and the older gentleman hesitantly reached forward to shake it.

"My name is Samantha Rose. I am here with my best girlfriend. It is my first trip to Aruba and certainly won't be the last."

"Pleased to meet you, Samantha. Do you have friends here at the Costa Linda that you are visiting?"

"No. I won a trip here for me and a friend. It has been a great escape from the pressures of my work in Chicago and a break from the winter weather, which has been bad this year. Where are you from?"

"I live in Connecticut, but work in Manhattan."

Samantha studied the man's face. He seemed familiar to her. She tried to recall whether she had met him previously.

"Excuse me, but you look familiar to me. Have we met?"

"I don't know, Samantha. What is it you do in Chicago?"

"I am a lawyer with the firm Gouge, Driller, and Hammer."

The old man threw back his head and laughed.

"That is funny, Miss. I taught Michael Gouge, and he articled for me. I am Benjamin Isaac. Most call me Benny, and you can too. I started the New York firm of Isaac, Bernstein, and Sax. We were counsel to a number of the Wall Street brokerages. Michael Gouge was a quick learn and excelled at the firm. I was personally selected by the Office of the President to handle some sensitive legal matters for the Department of Defense."

Samantha recalled where she had seen him before. His photo had graced the cover of the American Bar Association Journal and many press articles covering high-profile financial cases.

"It is an honor to meet you in person, Mr Isaacs."

"I told you to call me Benny. Just as well we aren't in court and you are defending some poor wretch against me. Mr. Isaacs indeed. It's Benny. Now let me buy you a coffee."

Armed with their coffees, they sat in the large wicker chairs on the patio facing the garden.

"So, Miss Samantha, are you seriously looking to purchase a unit here at Costa Linda?"

"This vacation has opened my eyes. I have lost the balance between working and enjoying life. High-pressure cases with clients transferring their problems onto me, a shattered personal life as a result of the betrayal of my lover, the loss of my father, and more. I need to refocus, and I think that if I had a place here in Aruba that would provide me with the incentive to change things. I wish my father was still alive. He was my best friend and guide in life. He would have loved it here."

"Well, when you summarize things like that, I can appreciate why Aruba may offer you respite from the stress we lawyers live with. I am sorry to hear of the loss of your Dad. What did he do?"

"He was Captain Owen Rose of the US Navy. He was lost while deployed on a mission. The circumstances have never been fully disclosed to my Mother and me. Every day I think of him and the influence he had on his family and friends."

A tear welled in her eye and spilled down her cheek. Benny Isaacs looked at her, unsure how to react. He sat back in shock.

"Samantha, there is something I must tell you. I led the inquiry into the unfortunate incident that took the lives of him and his crew. My involvement was never made public. The issues were so sensitive. I understand how difficult it must have been for you and your Mother, but trust me when I say the details needed to be kept secret. I hope that one day the whole matter will be declassified and you and millions will understand the sacrifice he made for mankind. I know these words do not replace the need to honor him, but I guarantee that if you knew the circumstances, you would accept things a lot easier."

"Why can't the truth be shared with us?"

"Officially, they will claim a matter of National Security. Believe me, it is a lot more than that. Captain Owen Rose died a hero, and one day it will be acknowledged."

A stillness surrounded them. Samantha sat sobbing quietly, while Benny Isaacs attempted to compose himself. The intensity of Samanthas' grief washed over him and brought back memories of Ruth, his beloved wife. He stood, went, and sat by her and hugged her. She lifted her tear-stained face and smiled at him.

"I am sorry. I'm meant to be a hardened lawyer devoid of emotion and capable of handling emotional events."

"My dear, at this advanced stage in my life, I understand human emotions a lot more than in my younger years. If you didn't have emotions, it would be abnormal. All that I read or was informed of regarding Captain Rose indicated he was an amazing man. You must be proud and carry on in a tradition that would make him proud. Now, shall we discuss the Costa Linda time share? Better still, would you be interested in seeing it? I must warn you that without Ruth around, my housekeeping is a little deficient."

"I would love to see it. I promise to look away from any little housekeeping issues."

They finished their coffees. Samantha composed herself, and they left and rode up in the elevator. Upon reaching his floor, they exited and walked along the external walkway to the end of the building. He opened the door and ushered her into a large open living area overlooking the ocean. To her right was a fully equipped kitchen. She walked to the door leading out to the patio and was amazed to see a BBQ constructed on the large deck.

"This has been my escape from exactly what you described for many years, but now it's time for me to let it go. It is one of the few 3-bedroom units. Walk around. Take your time."

Samantha went from room to room before finally taking a seat outside on the patio with Benny.

"It is perfect. I can see myself here with my mother and friends. Tell me more about timeshare ownership at Costa Linda."

Benny spent the next 15 minutes describing the ownership. Samantha absorbed the information like a sponge. When he finished, she sat quietly.

"What exactly will you be selling?"

"I purchased 2 weeks' ownership, but as a surprise for me, Ruth added a week. I will be selling all 3 weeks."

"I need to know the price you're looking for."

Benny looked pensive and sank his chin into his hand. He sat without responding for minutes and then spoke.

"I wish to be fair, and I would be happy to have someone like you purchase it. I know the enjoyment you will get from it. I have a suggestion, let's go down to the Management offices. I will ask what prices units have sold for in the past. I hope they have and will share that information. That will help me to set a price and assure you it is a fair price."

Benny informed the office of his plans, and after some convincing, was able to obtain a range of suggested prices. Within minutes, Samantha agreed on a price, and the deal was made.

"Benny, you have made me the happiest person. Now we need to handle the business end of the deal."

Details were provided, and Samantha arranged a banking transfer. They arranged to meet the next day after the financial transaction was completed and sign the transfer documents with the Costa Linda management.

Samantha left the Costa Linda ecstatic.

Satisfied, she returned to find both Jan and Sophia asleep on the loungers. She sat and lay back thinking about her experiences in Aruba.

The hours drifted by. The sun was close to setting. She woke up Jan and Sophia.

"Jan, this has been a great day and afternoon. Sophia and I need to return to our resort and freshen up. I intend to do something tonight that I never do at home. I am feeling lucky and want to visit a casino. Later, I will share a big surprise with you both."

They gathered up their belongings, returned the towels, and left to return to the Bucuti.

Chapter 18

Nightlife

The Casino

For weeks, the Aruban police had monitored and tailed a certain woman who was preying on older men at the Marriott Stellaris Casino. They knew who she was and where she lived. Even after weeks of surveillance, they were unable to identify her accomplices or how she was able to operate. They were confused. She had a system or someone on the inside advising her on who the wealthy targets were.

Antoine LaFortune had been assigned to the case. He had tracked her every movement and was determined to find who she was working with and the individuals involved. He was concerned about his objectivity, as he had developed a strong liking for her and her intelligence, and the way she operated. In his mind, she was a master criminal and someone to admire. Most crooks were dumb, he believed, but not this woman known only as Val. She was a professional con woman.

Late that afternoon, he had followed her up to the beach at Malmok.

On the beach, Val sat. The sky filled with golden and pink clouds as the sun dipped down to the horizon at the end of another tropical day. She loved the island's sunsets. Sitting on a bench above the sandy strip of beach, Antoine LaFortune sat watching her. For weeks, he had seen her go to the beach for sunset.

As dusk darkened to night, Val swept up her few possessions and headed to do what she knew best. Swindle the unattached wealthy gamblers at the Casino. Antoine watched her throw her things into her Hummer, which she had convinced a certain US politician to buy for her, provided she remained quiet. He climbed into his Mini and followed. He was intrigued. Her reputation in the Detective Division was well known. Many men who had been targeted by her and fleeced had arrived at the station wanting to complain, but Val knew the law. There were no grounds. She was as cunning as a fox. Most of the Detectives admired her cleverness, and more than several fantasized about a wild night with her. While she was a criminal, she was admired.

Back at the Bucuti resort, Jan insisted he would join Samantha and Sophia for their night out at the Casino and that he would be their chaperone. There was no resistance to his suggestion. Especially from Sophia.

" Tonight I am off duty. I need to return to my apartment and change into something more appropriate for an evening out. I will return in an hour to escort you ladies to the Casino. It's not often I get to spend the night enjoying something other than police work."

Antoine followed Val into the parking lot at the Marriott resort. It was packed. He watched as she circled it and, without hesitation, pulled into the area that was reserved for senior staff and management. This surprised him, as the resort management strictly enforced parking there. Anyone not authorized would be towed. He wondered how Val had the privilege to park there. Who in the resort management was she working with, he wondered?

He watched as she spun herself out of the driver's side door of the Hummer. It was a challenge for her. Val's small stature made stepping down from it difficult. She crossed over to the Casino entrance. He was surprised that she would go to the Casino wearing cut-off jeans and a shirt knotted together at the front, displaying her midriff and lots of skin. It was the first time he had seen her enter the Casino in such casual clothes. It was out of character for her. Normally, she wore something classy as she enticed the lonely older male gamblers. It triggered alarm bells in his head, and he wondered what was transpiring that would cause her to deviate from her normal routine. As he watched, she stopped and spoke for a while with one of the doormen. It was a long conversation. Antoine noted the man and decided that he would be taken in for questioning when they busted Val and her accomplices.

Antoine waited until she was inside, so his arrival in the Casino would not be noticed. He waited until a group of tourists was heading toward the entrance. He hurriedly left his car and merged in with the tourists, pretending to be one of them. He spoke to the men in the group as if they were long-time friends. Anyone watching the CCTV cameras live, or at a later date, would not see him as an on-duty cop. Inside the Casino, bells on slot machines rang as players won. The air was cold as the air conditioning dropped the temperature to a level the Casino operators were convinced would entice players to linger and play longer. He was pleased there was no smoking in the Casino. He peeled away from the tourists and buried himself in a group that had gathered around to watch a player winning at Roulette. He scanned the tables for Val. She was nowhere to be seen. He walked past the rows of slot machines. Again, she was not to be seen. He followed one of the drink waitresses, trying not to seem obvious, pretending he was looking for someone. He acted frustrated, looking for his non-existent partner, and faked a question to a waitress asking if she had seen a woman whose characteristics he made up.

He was about to leave when he noticed a cleverly concealed door to the back and left of the cashier's cage open, and Val walked out. Antoine was intrigued. In all the weeks he had watched her, nothing like this had ever happened. She walked slowly, not drawing attention to herself, and out the exit. He followed and pursued her to her Eagle Beach apartment. It was a fenced building with a security guard controlling access. He decided not to enter but to park across the road on the grass strip beside the entrance to the beach. From there, he could watch vehicles leaving. If she attempted to drive out, it would be easy to see her in the bright red Hummer.

He did not have to wait long. Fifteen minutes passed before she emerged, driving the Hummer. Antoine wheeled around in a U-turn and followed her. To his surprise, she drove into the entrance of the Hilton. She drove up to the reception entrance, stopped, and waited. She did not get out of the Hummer. A doorman approached her. He handed her an envelope and left. Antoine noted the man as he decided to also take him in for questioning.

Antoine wondered about the deviation from her normal pattern. He guessed something big was about to happen, but had no idea what it could be. He sat trying to decide whether to call for assistance. He wanted help with monitoring her movements and tracking the others she spoke with. He wanted other cops available to assist, as it appeared some imminent action was about to take place.

While sitting and watching, he was surprised when her door opened and, with the assistance of a parking valet, she stepped down from the Hummer.

Val walked across to a muscular blonde-haired man in his early forties, wearing an expensive tailored suit, and they headed for the entrance. He went by the name Kurt van Rheinhart. Dressed in her long black slinky dress, stiletto-heeled shoes, and with her long black hair flowing, she was the perfect accompaniment to the man. To the casual observer, they created the image of an affluent professional couple. In reality, they worked as a pair. He acted as a roper to find a target, and she moved in to swindle the victim. She had no hesitation or reservation in going with the victim to his room. She engaged in sexual performances that could result in heart failure in less healthy men. Several hotels had needed to replace complete bedroom furnishings after her wild trysts. It was an agreed-upon fact that he would only focus on older men who seemed fit, healthy, and were dropping lots of money. While Val was occupied, Kurt sympathetically listened to tales of woe from women who had either been abandoned by their wealthy husbands or who had abandoned them. He lavished attention on them and led them into an experience of fantasy. He was never rejected, and often the reward compensated for less-than-enjoyable encounters.

Now, Antoine was able to understand how she had confused the police for so long and who she was working with. The mystery was solved. All he needed to do was catch them in the act and have them arrested.

Neither he nor Val had any scruples.

The sun had set, and nightlife in Palm Beach buzzed. People were dressed both casually and in fancy style. The sidewalks were busy. Women stood at the street vendors' stalls examining dresses, scarves, jewelry, and tacky souvenirs. Husbands looked bored while waiting for the chance to slip away and visit one of the many bars.

Sophia had dressed for the occasion and proudly held Jan's arm. He was thrilled with her attention to him. Samantha watched and quietly approved that Sophia had finally established a relationship after the marital disaster she had endured. She wondered whether it would be just a vacation fling or whether something more serious could develop.

After walking the strip, they agreed to take a taxi up to the Marriott Stelaris Casino. Samantha preferred the look and atmosphere of the Stelaris.

Inside, Sophia headed to the slots, and for a short while, they laughed and joked as they consecutively won and lost. After an hour, Samantha decided to try her luck at one of the Blackjack tables. She joined a small group who were playing conservatively.

The dealer dealt her into the game. For a while, Samantha lost each hand, then her luck changed. The other players increased their bets as luck worked against the dealer. Samantha continued to amass her winnings.

Jan and Sophia stood and watched in awe as Samantha continually won. A buzz circulated about her winning, and an audience gathered to watch. Amongst the audience, Kurt stood deciding whether to play or to make a move on Samantha. He decided to wait for a pause in the game before attempting to engage her in conversation and commence his routine.

Antoine watched as Kurt moved closer to Samantha. He was shocked when he saw she was with Jan van der Brekel. He recognized him as a fellow officer. He carefully signaled Jan to follow him. Jan excused himself and followed Antoine to the washrooms.

After checking the stalls for other occupants, Antoine spoke.

"Jan, your friend is about to be set up by one of the masterminds behind the scheme of manipulating winners out of their winnings and more. They target both men and women, and often the victims are taken for more than just their winnings. We have a raid planned. I suggest you find a way to get your friends away from here. Can you get a message to her without it being obvious?"

"I will ask our mutual friend, Sophia, to distract her and follow her to the washroom. I will convince them it's time to leave."

Jan returned to the Blackjack table and took Sophia into his arms in a passionate embrace. It was a disguise to fool anyone watching them. Sophia responded in a manner Jan was least expecting. He whispered in Sophia's ear that they needed to leave in a hurry as a raid was scheduled. She froze momentarily, then faked a fainting spell. Samantha immediately stopped playing and cashed out.

Moments later, the three hurriedly walked to the concierge at the exit and requested a taxi.

As they entered the taxi, several marked police cars and a police van roared into the Casino entrance. Jan watched the action before commenting.

"That is a major raid. You are lucky to have escaped. Initially, they will detain many for questioning. Let's get back to your resort and away from all this activity. I think drinks on the balcony are in order."

Samantha laughed.

"But I will need to spend all of my winnings. The florins will be of no use to me back in Chicago."

Sophia saw the opportunity.

"That's not a problem. Tomorrow we will visit the D shop we have heard about. I am sure your problem with the money will easily be solved."

Jan nodded in agreement as they arrived back at the Bucuti. He had plans for the balance of the night with Sophia. Samantha was aware of the interaction between Sophia and Jan and was pleased.

Just before Jan left, he turned to them with a suggestion.

"Each morning before I leave to work, I try to get in some exercise. Tomorrow I plan to climb Mount Hooiberg early in the morning before it gets too hot. Why don't you join me?"

After a brief chat, they agreed. Jan offered to drive them to Mount Hooiberg.

Chapter 19

Day tripping

The early morning temperature had dropped from the intense heat of the previous day. Dressed in shorts and sneakers, they waited for Jan to arrive. In the lobby area, they chatted with the staff and mentioned their planned climb. The staff urged them to take some cold water.

"It's almost 600 steps to the top. You will need some water, and you must wear hats. The view from the top is panoramic. You won't regret the experience. You may question your sanity during the climb and wonder why you did it, but the feeling of conquering it is worth it. At the top, the view is unbeatable. You will see Aruba in its full glory – the blues of the Caribbean, the stark contrast of the rugged landscape dotted with cactus, the expanse of arid land, and the busy life of Oranjestad in the distance. It is a scene you will remember for your life.

Samantha and Sophia were questioning their decision when Jan arrived and bounded into the resort.

"Bon Dia. I have arranged to take a couple of vacation days. I have more ideas for things to do after Mount Hooiberg. After the climb and a small rest, I will take you to Aruba's famous Aloe factory, where you can see the Aloe Vera plantation and the plants processed to produce cosmetics. I suspect you will both purchase some of the products. We can then go for a casual lunch, after which we can visit the famous D Shop."

Samantha and Sophia stood dumbfounded.

"We are going to do all that in one day? Are you sure?"

Jan laughed as he held the door open for them.

"It's a small island, so it's easy to get to all the places."

Sophia made an exaggerated whine like a young girl.

"But I want to go to that D Shop and see all the fashions."

"Not with me. I'd rather be out arresting criminals than shopping. Especially for women's clothes. Not my idea of fun."

They all laughed, and Jan drove them inland until they connected with the Watty Vos Boulevard. Jan turned off the highway and threaded his way through a collection of rough roads in poor shape and some dirt roads before arriving at the base of Mount Hooiberg.

With apprehension, the ladies looked up to the summit.

"Are you sure we will make it up there and back?"

" We will climb at an easy pace. You will be fine and thank me afterwards. I estimate it will take us an hour to climb and return."

Sophia shot him a questioning look.

Jan examined Samantha's bruised and cut knee from the earlier police action at he lighthouse. The cut was healing, and a slight blueish purple bruise surrounded the cut. He proclaimed her good for the climb.

Samantha led the climb. At the halfway point, they stopped for a drink of water and to rest.

"I thought I was fit, but this has shown me otherwise. I will be increasing my trips to the gym when I am back in Chicago. Some of my clients will need to have their cases done at a normal pace. I have decided this trip to limit those long sixteen-hour days. I need to start enjoying my life again."

The sun beat down on them. Fortunately, a light wind was blowing and provided some relief from the heat and humidity.

They reached the top, and their breath was taken away by the scene. They stood looking in all directions and taking in the sights, and marveled at how the island's topography differed between the flat land near the ocean and the hills. The contrast surprised them.

They rested at the top for a while, then started the descent.

On the way down, Sophia proclaimed her legs had turned to jelly, as her leg muscles reacted to unaccustomed stress.

After the climb, they bundled into Jan's car. He blasted the air conditioning, and they headed off to explore the Aloe Factory and Museum.

It was still early in the morning when they arrived, ahead of the crowded tour buses. They entered the Factory through the store entrance. The scents of the many cosmetic products filled the air in the store. A young Aruban man approached them and told them he was the guide for their visit to the Factory and Museum. He led them upstairs, and before they started the tour, he gave them a history and description of the operation.

"Aloe has been in use for centuries. Its medicinal value was known and used back in the time of Nefertiti in ancient Egypt, and its medicinal use has been documented over the centuries and in more recent times. Christopher Columbus was reputed to have grown the plant in pots aboard his ships to treat the injuries and other ailments. The extract of Aloe Vera was commonly used as a laxative, amongst other things.

Aloe was introduced to Aruba in the early 1800s, and it was grown extensively all over the island. In 1890, Cornelius Eman recognized the commercial value of the plant and established Aruba Aloe Vera. Besides harvesting the resin from the plant, it was discovered that the Aloe oils possessed many beneficial effects on burns and skin.

We will start our tour with a visit outside to the plantation where the plant is grown."

They followed the guide out to a large dusty expanse of land covered with the distinctive shape of growing aloe plants. Samantha was amazed.

Back inside the Factory, the guide continued.

"After the aloe is cut, it is processed to extract the ingredients that are used in the products you will see in the store downstairs. In addition to the processing, you can see we have a testing laboratory to test and ensure the aloe is of the highest quality and the plants are disease-free. Another interesting fact is that aloe that is grown in Aruba, with our warm climate, produces almost twice the resin as aloe grown in different countries. We are proud of our company. It is world-renowned and employs us locals. It is an achievement for Aruba, as it is such a small island, and Aruba Aloe products are shipped around the world."

At the end of the tour, they both asked the guide many questions before descending on the store. Jan waited patiently outside. It seemed like an eternity before Samantha and Sophia emerged with bags full of products. Both were happy.

"While waiting out here in the sun, I developed a real thirst. There is somewhere special I will take you."

Jan laughed as he drove back along the coast to the north end of the island. At Malmok, he turned inland and drove to the entrance of the Tierra del Sol Golf Club. He drove up past large, impressive houses until he reached the top and parked.

"Jan, neither Sophia nor I play golf, plus we're not dressed for a place like this."

"Stop worrying and follow me."

They climbed a small set of stairs and entered a corridor leading to a restaurant where a friendly waitress greeted them.

" Bon Tardi. Welcome. Would you care to sit inside or outside?"

"I think the ladies would love it outside with that spectacular view."

The waitress escorted them through to the elegant outside patio. Samantha and Sophia stood admiring the expansive view over the golf greens. In the distance, they watched as the ocean crashed up against the shore, sending plumes of spray high into the air. The easterly wind caught the spray and carried it inland. On the manicured lawns, they watched hungry iguanas foraging in the grass and chasing each other for food. A flock of large, dark colored birds rested on a green close to the patio.

Samantha was enraptured by the scene.

"This is a magical view. I never expected to see something like this on a desert island. Aruba is so dry, yet the grounds are so green. I love that they retained groups of cacti around the course. It keeps the Aruban flavor."

The waitress seated them beside the glass railing so they could enjoy more of the view. A warm but refreshing breeze cooled the patio.

Jan decided to order drinks to start their late lunch. He studied the wine list and, after conferring with the ladies, ordered a fine chardonnay.

Samantha chose an order of avocado toast for the table to share and a Cobb Salad. Sophia selected a Club sandwich, and Jan decided on the Gourmet Cheeseburger.

Throughout lunch, Sophia dominated the conversation, excitedly recalling the adventures they had experienced since their arrival. Jan hung on every word. His eyes remained fixed on her. Samantha knew then that the relationship between Sophis and Jan was more than just a fleeting holiday fling. She was happy for Sophia but wondered how they could manage a long-distance relationship. She considered Sophia to be too active and lively to sit back and wait for someone.

Jan ordered another bottle of wine, and while the conversation continued, Samantha was uncharacteristically quiet. It was noticed by Jan.

"Samantha, you have been very quiet today. Is something bothering you? Are you feeling well? I am concerned. You seem withdrawn and in another world."

"No, Jan. Thank you for your concern. I guess it's time for me to be honest about something I did."

Sophia jumped in immediately, eager to learn more.

"OK. Tell me. Who is he? Where did you meet him? Will I get to meet him? Is he rich? Where does he live? Does he own one of those palatial residences at Malmok?"

She reflected for a minute, then continued.

"Oh, no. Has something bad happened? What have you done?"

Samantha reached over and took Sophia's hand.

"No, honey. It's nothing like that. Here is the surprise. I bought a 3-bedroom timeshare at the Costa Linda on the top floor. It will be my refuge away from the zoo that is my life in Chicago."

Sophia's jaw fell open, and Jan just stared at her.

"But how? We have been together since we got here. What tricks did you pull? Did you know about this before we left Chicago?"

"There is nothing strange or hidden. While you and Jan were dozing on Eagle Beach, I took a walk through the Costa Linda. While I was studying the rentals and resales postings at their management office, I met an older man, and we started chatting. It turns out we have a lot in common that I never knew about. He is a famous lawyer from New York. He trained the senior partner of our firm in Chicago. The real bombshell came when we were discussing our lives. His name is Benny Isaacs. He was appointed by the US President to handle certain legal matters for the Department of Defense. In fact, the major driving force behind his appointment was the terrible accident that took my father's life. Benny Isaacs handled the US government's case. We spoke, and I now appreciate some things I am not at liberty to discuss. His wife died recently, and since he is retiring, he decided to sell his Costa Linda unit. I visited it and it is ideal for me. I will be able to take my mother and certain friends on vacation with me."

Except for the continual murmuring of the wind, there was total silence.

Sophia broke the silence.

"Well, I hope I'm one of those friends. Anyway, congratulations. Can we see it before we leave?"

"Tomorrow I meet Benny to sign the transfer documents. I am sure he would agree for you to see it."

"Samantha, you are my best friend, and I do not want to offend you, but there is something I wish to ask. Jan and I need to discuss whether we have any sort of future together. This evening I would like to spend time alone with him. I hope you understand."

"I have been watching the two of you, and yes, I understand. I am not offended that you both want a little private time. Besides, tomorrow is our last day here."

"We will meet for breakfast. Thank you for being so understanding."

Light-hearted conversation continued through lunch. Both Jan and Sophia peppered Samantha with questions about the timeshare and her plans. Sophia magnanimously offered to occupy it if Samantha was unable to use it.

"Samantha, with all that high-profile work you do, I expect you will be promoted and so busy that you will be unable to visit it. I promise to take care of it for you."

They laughed.

"Ladies, the afternoon is slipping by. Against my better judgment, I will take you both to the D Shop and then back to the Bucuti."

Thirty minutes later, they walked into the store. The glass doors swung open, and they were visually assaulted by a dazzling and sparkling display of jewelry in front of them. To the left, and much to Sophia's delight, were racks of stylish shoes. Within minutes, she had selected several pairs to try on. Sensing a sale, a smartly dressed attendant in a classy black dress arrived to serve them. Jan groaned.

An hour later, Sophia sat surrounded by empty shoe boxes from the many samples she had tried. Beside her was a small pile of the ones she had decided to buy. The sales attendant worked at a frenzied pace, mentally calculating the commissions she would earn.

When they left the store, with Jan carrying many boxes, dusk had arrived. They drove back to the resort in high spirits.

At the resort, Samantha said goodbye to Jan before he and Sophia left to spend the evening at his apartment. She was happy that Sophia had found someone, but was concerned about the logistics of a long-distance romance.

Samantha retired to her room. She relaxed for several hours and found she was not tired. There was too much on her mind with the timeshare purchase, the thought of returning to the office, and facing the Terry Steele issue. She wished the life of the past week could continue indefinitely.

Uncharacteristically, she changed into a classy outfit and decided to visit the beach bar. She decided the distraction would erase her anxiety of returning to Chicago.

The bar was quiet. Several couples sat talking and listening to soft music. Samantha was considering returning to her room when a gregarious couple walked into the bar. They walked over to the bar and seated themselves next to Samantha.

"I'm Mike O'Doul, and this is Colleen. We're from Ireland. We're meant to be here on our honeymoon, but she's so damned sunburnt I can't get near her. Best birth control ever, I'd say. Well, we'll be saving a bunch of money on those condom things. That's bloody good as I'll have more money for me Guinness."

"Jesus, Mike. You need to blab to everyone about us? Your bollocks probably made her want to leave already. And what a lovely lass she seems to be. Now, because she's a deadly looker, you just sit down and shut up, or I'll need to tell you to Eff off. Leave me alone to meet this nice girl."

Samantha took an immediate liking to them. She introduced herself and was reduced to tears of laughter at the many tales they told. Hours went by, and with some regret, she wished them a good evening and, still chuckling, returned to her penthouse suite.

Chapter 20

Next day

Samantha sat alone, waiting for Sophia to join her for breakfast. She picked at her fruit bowl and sipped her fresh orange juice. It was unlike Sophia to be late. Samantha was concerned, as Sophia had left to spend the night at Jan's apartment.

Fifteen minutes later, a glum-looking Sophia joined her.

"Sophia. Good morning. What is wrong? You look sad."

"Last night did not go as I hoped. Maybe I expected too much."

Sophia sat and picked up a menu and ordered in a manner that indicated the conversation regarding last night was over.

Knowing Sophia as well as she did, Samantha decided to stay silent. She knew Sophia would eventually discuss what had happened. Minutes dragged by.

"Well, aren't you going to ask? Aren't you interested in your best friend's crisis?"

"Sophia, I respect your personal business and would never pry. It is entirely up to you if you wish to discuss it."

Sophia angrily shot back.

"So it's like that, is it? You want to use your lawyer façade with me?"

"No, Sophia. I can see you are upset, and I don't want to say or do anything to further upset you."

Samantha felt sorry for her and watched as tears started to fall down Sophia's cheeks.

"Come on, Sophia. You have only known Jan for less than a week."

"I know, but there was some sort of special bond that developed. I have never experienced that in my past relationships."

"Maybe it's because it happened here in Aruba, while you are in a paradise of sorts. Possibly your relaxed mental state and willingness to experience things new and exciting have affected your judgment."

"Samantha, you're being a bitch. I was thinking very clearly. I just didn't see or expect what happened."

"I am not trying to be a bitch. I am concerned for you as a friend who is obviously upset and hurting. If it will help, then share with me what has happened."

"He was a real gentleman. We went to his apartment and he served wine. I sat in his kitchen area while he fussed around preparing a meal for us. It was a delicious spaghetti carbonara. After dinner, we went out onto his balcony and chatted. I asked him about his life in the |Netherlands and why he had moved to Aruba. He went silent for a long while before responding. When he did it, it was a shock."

She paused and waited while a waiter poured them both fresh coffee.

"Samantha, he is married with two daughters."

Samantha replaced her coffee cup with such force that it spilled onto the white linen tablecloth.

"That is terrible. All this week, he has misled you."

"Not really. He explained the situation. He is separated and has filed for a divorce. He is seeking custody of the girls as he claims she is unfit to be their mother and has exposed them to an inappropriate situation. In the Netherlands, he owns a townhouse, and every month the house is professionally cleaned. On this particular occasion, the carpets were scheduled to be steam cleaned. Jan had been out with his daughters shopping and returned before the steam cleaner was finished. He walked in with his girls to find his wife spread-eagled on the bed and **in 'flagrante delicto'**. The carpets weren't the only things getting steamed."

Samantha was unable to hold back and released a loud, snorting laugh.

Sophia stopped and looked at her. She realized the humor and laughed.

"So, my dear Sophia, what are you going to do?"

"I need time to think about all of this. I am in Chicago. He is presently in Aruba but contemplating a return to Holland. I don't think I am prepared for a long-distance relationship. The trouble is, I really like him. In fact, I'd say I love him. Damn you, Samantha. It's all your fault. You shouldn't have invited me on this trip."

"Sophia, I am being lawyerly now and using my training to determine what you are not telling me. I think I know. You were intimate and slept with him."

Sophia's face turned crimson.

"I'm not a client, so turn off your lawyer act, and yes, it was heaven."

Sophia's mood calmed as she shared her situation with her best friend.

"Well, Sophia. I'm sure you will reason it out. In the meantime, this is our last day here on the island, so let's go crazy and enjoy."

"What do you suggest?"

"Well, considering the cold, snowy streets of Chicago, I am going to spend some time in those beautiful turquoise waters. After that, I intend to go back to the Bugaloe and have a late lunch and enjoy the live music they have there in the afternoon."

"Am I invited?"

They spent the day frolicking in the warm waters of the Caribbean and then travelled to the Bugaloe for a late lunch. The restaurant was busy, but a friendly waiter found a waterside table in an area where a constant breeze kept them cool.

Sophia's normal, cheery mood had returned.

"Samantha, I've never had one before, but before leaving Aruba, I am going to have one, and maybe more, depending on how it is. I'm having an Aruba Ariba."

"What the hell. I'm going for one as well."

Their lunch was light-hearted and fun. As the afternoon wore on, they ordered several Aruba Aribas. A solo singer arrived and started singing modern songs, and before long, both Samantha and Sophia were up dancing. When the singer started the song 'Jailhouse Rock', Sophia joined her. Walking around the restaurant with the microphone and taunting the men to sing verses.

The sun was setting when they decided to take a taxi back to their resort.

As the taxi pulled into the driveway of the Bucuti, they were surprised to see an Aruban Police car parked at the reception entrance. Sophia gasped when she walked in and saw Jan standing in the reception area in full police uniform. On seeing Sophia, he smiled and headed across to her. Samantha decided to quietly leave the scene.

"Sophia, I am sorry about how things ended last night. I want you to know I am really serious about us and this relationship. I really meant what I said about the end of my marriage. I understand that it is probably a lot for you to digest. Please take some time and consider it. If you wish for us to continue, please call me. I will come to Chicago, and then we can discuss the future. Now, since I am on duty, I must go with my partner, Otto, and keep the peace."

Sophia rushed up to Samantha's penthouse, bursting with the news.

"OK, now go and pack. We will have an early dinner. The VIP limo will be here early in the morning."

Chapter 21

Back to Reality

Goodbye Aruba (Well, almost)

Samantha met Sophia for breakfast at the Elements restaurant. They selected a shaded table on the beach.

"Sophia, I am sad to be leaving here today. We have done and seen a lot in 10 days. We have certainly had some interesting adventures."

They ate their breakfast in silence until it was time for the VIP. Limousine to take them to the airport. On the way back to her room, Samantha informed John, the concierge, that they were ready to leave. John immediately arranged for their luggage to be taken from their rooms.

Before returning the complimentary tablet that the Bucuti had provided for her stay, Samantha checked her messages. Most were junk offering invites to paid legal seminars, offers for books, adverts for concerts, but there was one message marked important. The message was from Tracy Brown, of the bank's PR firm. She opened the message:

'Hi Samantha. I hope you and Sophia had a great time in Aruba. Love to hear about it all when you return.

Today is your last day, and Clive Jonas asked me to contact you and advise that Henry will pick you up from your flight and take you to your home. You will be met at the arrivals exit by the gate.'

Samantha smiled. She quietly appreciated knowing that the arrival home would be less stressful. She was looking forward to seeing Henry again.

The VIP driver was waiting at reception to assist them with their luggage. In silence, they drove to the airport. Another young lady from VIP Service met and escorted them past check-in and through the procedures for immigration and customs. When they cleared, she took them to the VIP lounge at the airport and offered them food and drinks before leaving them.

They had almost two hours to kill before the flight. A young couple sat down in the lounge chairs next to them and struck up a conversation. The couple had honeymooned in Aruba and excitedly told them of their time on the island. Time flew by, and an attendant approached them to advise them that they needed to leave and board the flight.

After boarding the flight and while sitting in first class, the same young male flight attendant arrived and greeted them. He cheekily turned and said to Sophia:

"I think I have steaming hot buns for you today."

They all laughed, and he asked them whether they had enjoyed the trip to Aruba, as he served the champagne.

Soon they were airborne. Samantha looked out of the window and down to the outline of the rugged shore of the wild east coast of the island. As they climbed, clouds blocked her view. She turned to speak to Sophia and noticed tears on her face.

"Sophia, what is the problem?"

"I can't explain, but I feel sorry and sad to be leaving. I know it's silly, but something happened to me there."

"I feel the same way. What is it about the island that makes us feel like this? I am meant to be a hardened lawyer and resistant to emotions."

"But now you have an attachment to Aruba. You have a timeshare at Costa Linda."

She foraged in her bag and found a pack of tissues, which she handed to Sophia.

The flight droned on for hours before touching down in Chicago. As first-class passengers, they disembarked first and walked the narrow jetway into the main body of the airport.

Samantha gasped. Standing at the exit was Peter Hutton, dressed in expensive jeans, penny loafers, and a light blue shirt underneath a tailored light brown suede jacket. With his tanned features, piercing blue eyes, and swept-back light brown hair, he was the image of a model.

"Samantha, Sophia, welcome home."

"What are you doing here? I thought Henry was picking us up."

"Yes, he is. He is waiting in the car outside. They are strict on parking here, and besides wanting to see you, my coming helped him with parking and waiting. Let me help you retrieve your luggage, and we will have Henry drive you home."

Samantha was both flattered and surprised.

They stood making small talk while waiting for their luggage at the carousel. Ten minutes passed before they left the building and stood waiting for Henry to complete driving the circle, as he had been unable to stop and wait at the curb.

Samantha felt the cold air immediately. The sounds of hotel shuttle buses, parking cops blowing shrill whistles, people calling out names, and the general noise of passengers arriving and leaving the airport building seemed loud and amplified after the serenity she had experienced in Aruba. Again, she started to miss it.

Henry pulled up and jumped from the car.

"Welcome home, Miss Rose. Did you have a nice vacation? We will take Miss Sophia to her place first, and then to yours."

During the trip, Peter Hutton sat across from them and asked them about Aruba and the things they did.

After dropping Sophia at her home, Henry proceeded on to Samantha's condo. At the condo, Peter Hutton exited and assisted her with the luggage before Lionel, the concierge, came to help.

Samantha waited and turned to thank Peter, but before she could speak, he smiled at her and spoke.

"Samantha, I find there is something special about you, and I would like to get to know you better. Will you join me for dinner tomorrow evening?"

She was shocked and accepted the invitation.

"Good. Tomorrow evening I will pick you up at 7:30."

Samantha stood and wondered if this was the start of a new chapter in her life.

www.ingramcontent.com/pod-product-compliance
Lightning Source LLC
LaVergne TN
LVHW091551060526
838200LV00036B/790